WHAT TO DO IF YOUR PRESIDENT IS A TRAITOR

By
Abraham Roosevelt Reagan

Let's Make America Good Again

The cause of America is the cause of all mankind.

From Thomas Paine's Revolutionary 1776 Pamphlet

Common Sense

CHAPTER ONE

Our President Is Probably a Traitor

Think carefully about those words. For a moment try to suspend all prejudice and preconceived notions. I know this is a challenge. Ignore your allegiance to any political party or cause. Consider that these words may well be true and ponder carefully their frightening implications. What if our President is a traitor to the United States of America and the noble ideals to which most Americans aspire?

It is important to understand what I mean by the word "traitor". The Merriam-Webster Dictionary defines traitor as "one who betrays another's trust or is false to an obligation or duty". It further defines a traitor as "one who commits treason". The crime of treason is the only crime mentioned in the U.S. Constitution. Article Three, Section Three defines treason as " . . . levying War against them, or in adhering to their Enemies, giving them Aid and Comfort".

It is not my intent here to dwell on the question of the potential criminality of the actions of Trump. I use the word traitor in this work based upon my profound view that Donald Trump has betrayed the very norms and institutions upon which our country was founded. I will detail herein why I believe he has betrayed our country and its citizens with every vicious slur and lie he has spoken or tweeted, intent on instilling fear and undermining the comity among our citizens: the common civility through which our community of diverse and disparate Americans can coexist in a peaceful and respectful environment. That is the miracle of our Founding Fathers' great experiment.

I will further detail why I believe Trump is a traitor who has betrayed, and continues to betray, the very foundations of our democracy, beginning most importantly with his unrelenting attack on our First Amendment's guarantee of a free and independent press as well as his ongoing subversion of our sacred electoral process. Whether or not we find that Trump was a willing accomplice in Russia's hacking of our 2016 national election we know for certain that he has been unwilling to take any affirmative action to protect our country from further attack. Astonishingly, in this regard the

Republican Congress (particularly the House of Representatives) has been a more than a willing ally in Trump's malignant neglect. There is no more vital organ of our democracy than our system of free, independent, and secure elections.

No bombs were dropped, nor bullets fired. Nonetheless, Russia attacked the United States by sabotaging the integrity of our elections. Russia continues to engage in this vicious subversion of our democracy. Trump's failure to safeguard our electoral process is a blatant violation of his presidential oath of office to "preserve, protect and defend the Constitution of the United States."

Since the election of Donald Trump there has not been a day (sometimes not a waking hour) that I have not worried about the irreparable injury that this vile man has done and will continue to do to our culture, our democracy, and our daily way of life. I have repeatedly wondered what I can do to help combat this flagrant assault on America. Of course, I will vote and encourage others to vote. I always have. But that is not enough. This is different.

As I thought about the helpful actions I might take in this most challenging time, I was reminded of Thomas Paine's historic pamphlet of the American Revolution, *Common Sense*. It was a call to arms: a coherent and passionate argument for the creation of an American nation independent from the autocratic rule of the British monarchy. (How odd it is that we have elected a President who openly admires murderous tyrants.) Paine's pamphlet laid out the case against King George and argued for a vision for a representative form of government. That argument was refined and enlightened in the ensuing months of debate in 1776, culminating in Thomas Jefferson's timeless declaration, "that all men are created equal, that they are endowed by their Creator with certain unalienable rights, that among these are life, liberty and the pursuit of happiness."

Inspired by the literal meaning of the title of Paine's work *Common Sense,* I have endeavored to publish this "pamphlet" with two goals in mind. First, I wish to summarize simply and coherently (and hopefully profoundly and urgently) some of the most salient facts that overwhelmingly and logically support my finding of Trump's malice toward the institutions of democracy, the civility of our culture, and the protections of our health and safety, both at home and abroad. Second and most importantly, my purpose in this writing is a call to action among our citizens to bring about a change in our state and federal legislatures (as well as the Presidency) beginning with the national elections this November, just three brief months away. Lifetime Republican (until this year) Steven Schmidt (John McCain's Presidential Campaign Chairman) recently, solemnly declared this is the "most important midterm in American history." There truly is no time like the present. I urge you to begin your volunteer work *immediately*, even before you finish reading this work. (If you are so inclined take a brief look now at Chapter VI and visit the links to organizations and campaigns that can use your help.)

I am not just writing about what Trump refers to as the "Russier thing." I will address the compelling evidence of Trump's complicity in the Russian hacking of our democracy and his unwillingness to take any action to protect our country from further attack. I will summarily detail the facts that I believe can leave us with no other rational conclusion than, at a minimum, Trump is complicit in the Russian attack on our democracy and is likely a willing participant in Moscow's designs.

However, there is more. Much more.

- He is a traitor to "everything for which our country stands."[1]
- He is a traitor to the Constitution and the Bill of Rights.

- He is a traitor to our long recognized moral and religious values and to every standard of common decency. He's a vulgar and narcissistic compulsive liar who has coarsened the conversation in our country, sowing discontent and hateful partisanship, and even suborning white nationalist hate groups. Even more shockingly (assuming one can be further alarmed by anything Trump might say or do), he has shamefully sanctioned the systematic imprisonment of terrified immigrant families seeking asylum (a legal act through ports of entry under U.S. law[2]) from terrorizing gangs in Central America. (Trump likes to refer to these desperate souls as "infesting" America, reminding us of other vile metaphors and propaganda conjured by murderous tyrants during the Twentieth Century.[3]) In a breathtakingly cruel and irreparably damaging act, he has separated children, including toddlers and breast-feeding infants, from their mothers and fathers. This is not the American ideal I grew up revering.

- He is a traitor to our most important democratic institutions, including a free and independent press, a fair and impartial judiciary, and a strong and independent Justice Department.

- He is a traitor to the institutions of government that keep our beautiful country and us safe and that protect our water, air, food and drugs.

- He is a traitor to America's standing in the world: that "shining city on a hill" that has been a beacon of the democratic ideal for over two centuries. This is *OUR PRESIDENT*. While he defames and disparages our most important traditional allies (countries such as England, Germany, France and Canada, with whom we have forged the most powerful, 70-year, post-World War II alliance against the rise of world terror and totalitarianism) he has literally and figuratively embraced the world's most notorious tyrants. He is a man who single-handedly has done more to undermine America's international prestige (perhaps irreparably) belying what Thomas Paine first declared, "The cause of America is the cause of all mankind." Vladimir Putin is sleeping well these nights.

In addition to shining a light on Trump's profound disloyalty and malice, this work questions why so many of us have been complicit in his scheme to disrupt American democracy: a plan clothed in the wardrobe of tyrants. Cleverly, Trump has implicitly bribed single-issue voters to suspend all good sense and probity in favor of achieving their primary goals, perhaps sacrificing the very foundations of American constitutional government and freedom in the service of their own selfish interests.

- Why do sincerely religious people rationalize their toleration of Trump's vulgar bullying, promiscuous philandering, as well as his instigation of hate, fear and violence?

- Why do Americans who proudly salute the flag and all it is supposed to stand for sanction the "leadership" of a man who has professed his gaudy admiration of tyrants and murderers, past and present?

- Why do politicians who were historically and profoundly suspicious of Soviet Russia's totalitarianism tolerate Trump's love affair with Vladimir Putin, a former KGB leader and a despot who orders the killing of his opponents and journalists and who has led the attack on our democracy?

- Why do gun owners who so eagerly tout the Second Amendment as their sacred Constitutional right so readily abandon the other hallmarks of our Bill of Rights and willingly tolerate Trump's relentless attacks on our free and independent press?

- Why do hardworking, blue-collar Americans support and trust a man (a transparent conman and carnival barker at that) who pretends to be their ally but is working quietly to destroy their best interests. "Pay no attention to what is happening behind the curtain."

Certainly, the people of the United States have not always abided by the ideals to which we claim to aspire. One need not be a historian to recognize the irony in some of our noble declarations. The Preamble to our Constitution (ratified in 1789) begins with the phrase "We the *People* of the United States" and yet in 1790 almost 18% of our inhabitants were African slaves: not "people" but mere chattel.[4] Those slaves must have wondered what the phrase to "secure the Blessings of Liberty" actually meant.

It is not necessary for me to list more examples of our country's many failings. The point is that in spite of them, often after great struggle, we have returned to those ideals and achieved immeasurable triumphs: a fact that has not been lost on the citizens of the world. "There is nothing that is wrong with America that we cannot fix with what is right about America."[5]

- In the 1860s we fought a bloodstained Civil War in large part due to the tormenting issue of slavery. Thank you, President Lincoln.

- In the 1940s we helped free the world of the brutal Axis Powers and notably, rather than entering Germany and Japan as imperial conquerors, we helped rebuild those nations to become free, democratic neighbors. Thank you, Presidents Roosevelt, Truman and Eisenhower.

- In 1964 and 1965, a time in our very recent history when, unbelievably, African Americans remained segregated by law (primarily in the south), we passed the Civil Rights and

Voting Rights Acts aimed at ending that profanity. Thank you, Dr. Martin Luther King Jr., President Johnson and President Kennedy.

When did cruelty become a national aspiration? When did we begin to applaud Presidents who were mongers of violence and hate? When again will a President enlist us to be "touched . . . by the better angels of our nature" as President Lincoln so poetically expressed in his First Inaugural Address?

So, what are we going to do? What actions are we prepared to take to protect our country from this man and the considerable damage he has wrought and will continue to wreak? That is the ultimate aim of this primer. It is a call for the armaments of society, metaphorically speaking, to render emergency aid to our suffering democracy before it is too late. It is intended to help wake up America and help us reframe the narrative in simple terms, exposing Trump for the dangerous demagogue that he is. It is a call for action with salient information regarding some of the tools available to all of us as voters and concerned citizens.

This is not a time to sit idly by. This is not a time to merely watch TV and complain. We must *all* volunteer. It is a time for civic involvement in energizing your families, friends and community to vote, to call and write their representatives, and to work for change. It is a time for engaging others in respectful discussion and debate, to weigh and evaluate the opinions and supporting facts presented here. Most importantly, it is a time to volunteer for state and federal political campaigns, even from afar, by volunteering in any way possible during these coming midterm elections, particularly in jurisdictions with important Congressional races.

Volunteering does not require that you learn how to debate all the issues or that you engage in arguments with another voter aimed at changing his or her mind. There are jobs for everyone, even the most introverted among us.

It is a time to march. This is not a trivial idea or plea. During the civil rights movement Americans of good conscience marched peacefully and ushered in the Civil Rights and Voting Rights Acts. Americans marched and sat in by the millions to help end the war in Vietnam. Women are now marching for their equality. Students from Parkland Florida are leading marches and a movement for sane gun safety in America. Citizens are marching to end the cruel internment of immigrants seeking safety for their families. When did *you* last march? When did *you* last commit yourself to a worthwhile cause, simply placing one foot in front of the other, one step at a time?

A great deal has been said about the solemnity of standing for the National Anthem. It's a song about the symbolic nature of our flag that "so proudly we hailed at the twilight's last gleaming." As children in school we pledged allegiance to that flag. The anthem and that allegiance should not be hollow declarations. We don't pledge allegiance to a mere colorful cloth banner. And we certainly don't pledge allegiance to one man -- or any man or woman for that matter. We pledge allegiance "to the *Republic* for which it stands", a republic with "liberty and justice for *all.*" Are we truly prepared to honor that pledge?

In the words of Simon and Garfunkel, "Where have you gone Joe DiMaggio? Our nation turns its lonely eyes to you." We're looking for a hero: a charismatic, talented figure who can lead us out of this nightmare. That person may or may not arrive this fall. Or in 2020. Right now, each one of us must be compelled to take up the task, one positive action, one step, one vote at a time.

Heed this clairvoyant warning written by French political scientist and historian Alexis de Tocqueville almost two hundred years ago in his work *Democracy in America*: "America is great because she is good. If America ceases to be good, America will cease to be great."

It is time to make America good again.

CHAPTER TWO

Recognizing the Problem – The Case Against
Donald Trump

If he walks like a duck . . .

I think we all suffer from the same affliction. Let's call it "Convenient Rationalization." Actually, a more honest description would be "Selfish Rationalization." I went a bit easy on Bill Clinton when he was impeached for lying under oath about sex. I couldn't bring myself to support his removal from office perhaps in part because I agreed with many of his political positions. I am certain many San Francisco Giant fans rationalized Barry Bonds' obvious use of performance enhancing drugs while cheering his 73-homerun season. I imagine a common fan's rationalization might have typically been, "He may be a cheater, but he's *our* cheater . . . and don't they all cheat?!"

In the words of California Republican Congressman Duncan Hunter, referring to Donald Trump, "He's an asshole, but he's our asshole."[6]

Can we count on Americans to do the right thing? During the Watergate era Republicans in Congress were generally supportive of Richard Nixon from the time of the famed Watergate break-in until the eve of Nixon's resignation. Only in the end did some key senators take the morally correct action and help end the reign of the corrupt Nixon Presidency. Of course, it was *only* when faced with the damning evidence of the "smoking gun tapes."[7] One key difference between then and now is the fact that during the Nixon presidency, the Democrats controlled both houses of Congress and were able to initiate a robust investigative process. (Remember the coming midterm elections?)

It is my opinion that we are confronting a moral and constitutional crisis in America unlike anything I have seen in my lifetime. In my view, what we confront today in Trump's world is exponentially more dangerous than the Nixon break-in and cover-up, and certainly Bill Clinton lying about sex (for which he was impeached) bears no rational relationship to the scores of Trump misdeeds. Not only have we already had an electronic break-in, it was perpetrated by a foreign enemy and is *still going on.* Not only does Trump lie about sex: he is a pathological liar by every objective measure.[8]

This is no time for Selfish Rationalization. We must believe our own eyes. We must trust the undisputed facts. If our President walks like a duck, talks like a duck, and acts like a duck, in all probability he also has webbed feet. In this case the "duck" of which I'm writing (the central premise of the urgency for immediate action) is that our President is a traitor to the fundamental principles of American democracy and, in my view, is probably a traitor to the country, either knowingly or at the very least complicitly. He has unapologetically facilitated the ongoing Russian attack on our republic. When it comes to Putin's Russia, Donald Trump is the "Enabler-In-Chief." The undisputed facts don't support any other logical conclusion.

If Putin has a playbook for destabilizing Western democracies he could not have found a more loyal servant to his schemes than our President. In terms of the actions we must take, does it really matter if Trump is Putin's willing protagonist or his pliable village idiot? The urgency is the same.

There is a principle in science that when confronted with compelling facts the simplest explanation is probably the correct one.[9] If your patient has a runny nose and a cough he's probably got a cold and not Dengue Fever. *Common sense.*

In the law there is a similar principle.[10] "The thing speaks for itself." In the case of Donald Trump we must force ourselves to admit that the simplest explanation for his actions is, in all probability, the correct one. His actions quite literally speak for themselves.

Here are a number of illustrations that I argue support my premise that Donald Trump is a traitor to the highest ideals and values of our country.

1. Donald Trump has an alarming affection for dictators, tyrants and murderers, past and present.

There are a plethora of examples (Turkey, the Philippines, China, Russia, Egypt, Saudi Arabia, etc.) of Trump's declarations of admiration for world despots, Vladimir Putin being the top of the list. If anything, Trump is a master of stagecraft and self-promotion. Have any of us envisioned our flag being waved proudly along side the flag of North Korea?[11] Give Trump a red carpet and a military band and he'll gladly alter US foreign policy to show appreciation for the symbolic "praise" of his band of "adoring" autocratic brothers.

At every mile of Trump's marathon of political malfeasance[12] he has taken the lane that most suits the worldview and interests of Vladimir Putin. Trump will not pass up an opportunity to rationalize or excuse Putin's actions. Here is a sample from an interview with Bill O'Reilly (remember him) from last year:

> *O'Reilly: Do you respect Putin?*
> *Trump: I do respect him . . .*
> *O'Reilly: Do you? Why?*
> *Trump: Well, I respect a lot of people . . .*
> *O'Reilly: But he's a killer though. Putin's a killer.*
> *Trump: There are a lot of killers. We've got a lot of killers. What do you think – . . . .*
> *You think our country's so innocent?*
> *O'Reilly: I don't know any government leaders that are killers.*
> *Trump: . . . . A lot of killers around, believe me.[13]*

2. Our President has shown a shocking antipathy toward our democratically elected closest allies while remaining steadfast in his unwillingness to contradict Vladimir Putin.

He has done this repeatedly: not only during his campaign but, even more disturbingly, he has doubled down on this disgraceful malice while clothed in the robes of the office of the President. Trump's despicable conduct toward our allies at the G-7 conference in Canada in June is only the most recent example. In early July he succeeded in offending our most strategic allies at the annual NATO summit in Europe followed two days later by sabotaging English Prime Minister Teresa May's government on the eve of a state dinner at which Trump was the guest of honor.[14]

If ever there was an opportunity to juxtapose Trump's gaudy embrace of dictator and murderer Vladimir Putin with Trump's distasteful malice towards our country's most important, historic allies and to succinctly expose what I believe is Trump's treasonous intent, that opportunity arose during a few days in July 2018. In an interview in Scotland shortly after the above-mentioned disastrous NATO Summit, a reporter asked Trump to identify his biggest foes. The *first* response Trump gave was that the European Union was one of our foes.[15] Around the same time the United States Justice Department filed a criminal indictment against twelve specifically named Russian intelligence officers. The details of the indictment were stunning in their precision. They support what the United States intelligence community has unanimously concluded during the last year and a half: that the Russians systematically hacked our 2016 Presidential election, intent on insuring the victory of Donald Trump.[16]

Just a few days later, Trump met with Putin in Helsinki, Finland. Incredibly, during the joint press conference that followed the Putin/Trump summit, Trump sided with Putin and his hollow denial of meddling in our election, contrary to the finding of our own intelligence services and top law enforcement officials. Trump noted, "I have President Putin, he just said it's not Russia." Trump continued, "I will say this: I don't see any reason why it would be."[17]

Trump, like all Presidents before him, took an oath of office whereby he promised to "preserve, protect and defend the Constitution of the United States."[18] At every opportunity Trump has chosen to violate that oath. He proudly defends Putin while attacking and undermining the most important institutions of American democracy, including the Justice Department: the guardian of America from threats, both domestic and foreign.

John Brennan, former head of the Central Intelligence Agency, in response to Trump's pathetic display in Helsinki, said it best when he wrote:

> Donald Trump's press conference performance in Helsinki rises to & exceeds the threshold of 'high crimes & misdemeanors . . . . It was nothing short of treasonous. Not only were Trump's comments imbecilic, he is wholly in the pocket of Putin. Republican Patriots: Where are you???[19]

3. There is no other rational explanation but that Trump is a traitor to American democratic values.

The fact that Trump is infatuated with despots, old and new, and has shown a remarkably sanguine ability to disrespect our democratic friends, should be sufficient cause for overwhelming concern. After all, he is President of the United States. But there is more. Much more.

Throughout history tyrants have been able to come to power (often peacefully after being duly elected to office) and stay in power by systematically attacking and controlling the levers and institutions of republican, representative government by following a fairly consistent and effective pattern.

a. Despots attack and take ultimate control of media (press, radio, TV, Internet).

The tactics are aimed at controlling the message with their own "facts" while undermining and/or eliminating the truth tellers. The use of propaganda to mislead the public has been classically employed in dictatorships both historically and currently.[20] Trump's systematic attack on our free press has been unrelenting and aligns perfectly with previous and current despots' devilish designs. Trump has incessantly repeated his false mantra "fake news" since he began his campaign, even audaciously calling the American media the "enemy of the American people."[21] Do we have to be constitutional scholars to remember the First Amendment protections for our free and independent press? He has even suggested the idea of jailing journalists and hardening libel laws.[22]

b. Tyrants attack artists and intellectuals.

By experience and temperament, artists and intellectuals are usually talented, informed and often charismatic and influential. Despots try to marginalize and/or eliminate these voices to the extent that they oppose the power and prestige of the tyrant.[23] This can be done modestly by labeling them "elite", as Trump likes to do,[24] ("they think they're better than you") or, more maliciously, by imprisonment or even murder.[25]

This quote from an LA Times article highlights Trump's methodology:

> When Trump ally and National Rifle Assn.
> President Wayne LaPierre teed off . . . on
> America's greatest domestic threats, he cited
> not homegrown terrorists but what he termed
> "the three most dangerous voices in
> America: academic elites, political elites,
> and media elites."
>
> Yet for Trump and his allies, a war on elites
> has been central to the campaign which put
> him in the presidency . . . . Trump has taken
> particular aim at entities that could counter
> his power, which has helped stoke the ardor
> of his political backers.
>
> Among his targets so far: the government's
> intelligence agencies, the media, foreign
> allies, the Department of Justice,
> establishment politicians, scientists and the
> Congressional Budget Office. The last has
> played a large role in raising questions about
> Republican proposals to repeal and replace
> Obamacare, leading to a furious White
> House assault on its competence.[26]

The irony of Trump's leadership against American "elites" is that he is by his own account a boastful billionaire, who plasters his name on tall buildings and lives a lavish lifestyle in gold-gilded salons.

c. Dictators attack and/or eliminate and replace the referees (i.e. the judges, police, and prosecutors.)[27]

Trump's malice toward judges is well documented, most notoriously his attack on Judge Gonzalo Curiel (an American born citizen of Mexican heritage) in his Trump University lawsuit. (Did anyone notice Trump's settlement with the plaintiffs in that case on the eve of trial?) All the while Trump is appointing a legion of new federal judges who may well be sympathetic to his worldview.

Even more distressing has been Trump's (and his sycophantic supporters in the Republican Party - particularly in the House of Representatives[28]) relentless attacks on what had been our most respected law enforcement agency, the F.B.I. Concurrently, he has engaged in a campaign to defame the members of the Justice Department and Special Counsel Robert Mueller's team and their discrete investigation into Russian tampering in our election.[29] His attacks on Robert Mueller,[30] a war hero, a conservative Republican, and a lifetime servant to the cause of justice in the United States,[31] are despicable. There is perhaps no other law enforcement official in the country with a more impressive and impeccable record of service. The sad fact is this persistent libel has been effective in shaping a significant portion of public opinion, particularly in the Republican Party.

> **d. Trump, like other despots before him, seeks to undermine faith in the democratic process.**

Throughout his campaign Trump called the "system rigged."[32] He even left doubt that he would accept the outcome of the election. His systematic slander of the Justice Department and related agencies is one more tragic example of Trump's campaign to sabotage the public's faith in our democratic institutions and the patient guarantee of due process in all legal matters.

> **e. Autocrats create scapegoats through hatred, greed and fear, through prejudice and racism, and by further instigating anger with malicious calls to violence.[33]**

Lest we forget, Donald Trump's original rise to national political prominence was enabled by his "leadership" role in the blatantly racist *Birther Movement*. He began his Presidential campaign by calling Mexican immigrants "killers and rapists."[34] He blatantly lied when he pretended not knowing who David Duke was (white supremacist and former notorious Grand Wizard of the Ku Klux Klan).[35] Trump's declarations in the aftermath of vile, torchlight demonstrations in Charlottesville,[36] reminiscent of Nazi thugs, were shocking, despicable and racist. He and his minions have called for the jailing of his opponents, most notably Hillary Clinton and James Comey. A brief visit to youtube.com will illuminate Trump's numerous calls to violence against citizens.[37]

And how many of us noticed in 2017, when Turkey's tyrannical President Erdogan's thugs beat up peaceful protestors in Washington, DC (yes, our nation's capital) that our "President" remained shamefully silent.[38] This stands in stark contrast to the calls of past presidents for Americans to do the morally right thing in the shadow of indefensible attacks on our democracy and human decency.

Steve Schmidt, lifetime Republican (until recently) and Chairman of John McCain's 2008 presidential campaign, has been one of the most articulate and thoughtful critics of the Trump fiasco.[39] He has noted common themes in Trump's actions and words that parallel and reinforce many of the patterns and arguments I summarized above. Schmidt is truly alarmed. In an appearance on

Chris Hayes' MSNBC show on June 26, 2018 Mr. Schmidt outlined five behaviors exhibited by Trump that Schmidt defines as the "hallmarks" of totalitarianism:[40]

> One. He incites fervor in a base through constant lying.
>
> Two. He scapegoats minority populations and he affixes blame for complex problems to them and them alone.
>
> Three. He alleges conspiracies that are hidden and nefarious and linked to those scapegoated populations.
>
> Four. He spreads a sense of victimization among those fervent supporters. And,
>
> Five. He asserts the need to exert unprecedented power to protect his victim class from the conspiracies and the scapegoated populations.

We ignore the ominous warnings of this rational, brilliant *conservative Republican* at our collective peril. I strongly urge you to view the Schmidt interview. And I repeat his plaintive appeal that this is the "most important midterm in American history."

CHAPTER THREE

Why I Believe Trump May Be the Worst Traitor in the History of the United States

There is no better rational explanation than that Trump is most likely a willing participant, or at a minimum is unwittingly complicit (I think this is being overly generous), in the Russian attack on our democracy.

Throughout my life I have never been a conspiracy theorist. I'd like to believe that I am moderate and objective in my political views, so I don't make these charges against Donald Trump idly without having given them considerable deliberation. However, the facts do quack for themselves.

I alluded earlier to the legal axiom of *res ipsa loquitor*: "The thing speaks for itself." Applying this maxim there are a class of civil cases where the burden of proof *shifts* to the "accused"[41] to prove that he/she did *not* commit the alleged wrong.[42] The facts surrounding every aspect of Trump's statements and actions are such that they speak for themselves by any reasonable explanation.

The overwhelming, undisputed evidence of Trump's complicity with Russia demands that he has the burden to prove his innocence. Trump's statements and conduct (or lack thereof) cannot otherwise be logically reconciled. Here is a summary of the evidence:

1. *Trump has relentlessly attacked Mueller and his investigation.*

Trump has consistently attacked the investigation into Russia's interference in our election and refused to accept the unanimous conclusions of our national security apparatus. Most troubling, he has failed to take action to protect our future elections or to similarly offer help to our allies in Europe who face similar assaults from the Russians.[43]

2. Trump's has failed to produce his long-promised tax returns.

Trump's financial history is well documented from his bankruptcy failures in Atlantic City to his close ties to Russian money.[44] Just ask Donald Trump Jr.[45], who in 2008 stated:

> In terms of high-end product influx into the US,
> Russians make up a pretty disproportionate cross-
> section of a lot of our assets . . . . Say, in Dubai, and
> certainly with our project in SoHo, and anywhere in
> New York. We see a lot of money pouring in from
> Russia.

And that was before Trump's infamous visit to Moscow in 2013 where he produced the Miss Universe Pageant.

Does anyone remember Trump's promise to produce his tax returns?[46] Why is he so unwilling to provide full disclosure to the American public? Is it because those returns may disclose the identity of creditors to whom Trump owes money as well as his other economic entanglements? Trump's financial landscape is littered with powerful inferences of Russian influence and possible extortion.

3. Mueller's investigation has already produced numerous results.

In spite of Trump's repeated claims that the Mueller investigation is a witch hunt and a hoax, and even though Mueller has been excruciatingly discrete in maintaining the integrity and confidentiality of his investigation, a number of Trump's former campaign members (including Paul Manafort, his former campaign chair) have been convicted or charged.[47] The number of Trump associates and campaign officials who actually met with Russians, in spite of testifying and/or making statements to the contrary (think Attorney General Jeff Sessions[48]), is startling.[49] Trump essentially admitted in a TV interview that he fired Comey because of the Russian probe.[50] Add to this Trump's hiring of Manafort as his campaign manager. Manafort's history and reputation as a sleazy international player in bed with Russian interests was one of Washington's worst kept secrets.[51] Who in this country is comfortable with a person who would make such a choice for the most important position in his presidential campaign? *Ironically* Trump is the same man who repeatedly called for "draining the swamp."[52] It looks like he has been satisfied with draining the water from the swamp but embracing all the denizens who dwelled there.[53]

4. *Trump has supported Putin and Russia's end goals at every turn.*

We should all be shocked by Trump's unabashed support of Vladimir Putin and Putin's well-known international designs. Regretfully, Trump's effective tactic of making outlandish tweets and statements on a daily basis (often even hourly) instead has us *shell*-shocked. Are we really becoming numbed to the frightening realities that our President may be the worst traitor in American history? Again, the best explanation for Trump's actions and policies regarding Russia is the obvious one: Trump is Putin's puppet, either by volition or stupidity or both. Why has Trump systematically disrupted our relationships with Western European and other NATO allies? Why is he threatening to withdraw American troops from Germany and the Far East? Why is Trump withdrawing America from our carefully nourished international political and economic relations? Why has Trump decimated the State Department, the agency of our country that is tasked with building and sustaining international relations and avoiding conflict? Why has Trump advanced the cause of fossil fuels and demeaned the emergence of alternative energy technologies?

My last question may be answered by Trump's clever endorsement of one-issue interests (in this case the fossil fuel industry) as summarized below. However, could his adoration of coal and other carbon-based fuels also be attributable to the fact that other than its Cold War military, Russia's only other major international asset is its robust oil and gas industry? Even with its vast energy reserves the Russian economy is much smaller than that of the state of California.[54] The somewhat meager and linear Russian economy is in a co-dependent relationship with the price of oil.[55] Trump's antagonism to alternative fuels, epitomized by his pulling out of the Paris Accords and his songs of praise for the non-existent "clean coal",[56] only encourages our reliance on fossil fuels and in turn supports the increase in gas and oil prices, favorable to sustaining Putin's grip on his abiding, Russian population.

CHAPTER FOUR

Everyone's Responsible For This Mess . . .
To Some Degree . . .

(. . . EXCEPT FOR DONALD TRUMP WHO IS <u>NEVER</u> TO BLAME . . . FOR ANYTHING[57])

Selfish Rationalization

Cleverly, Trump (with the aid of Russian hackers and the willing assistance of most members of the Republican Congress) has appealed to one-issue groups, "Selfish Rationalizers", who have been willing to sell their souls (or, in this case, to barter their willingness to protect the American republic) for the sake of one overriding interest.[58] Trump, who is amoral *at best*, probably does not care much about the agendas of these willing, self-interested followers. He will gladly oblige them so long as they will pledge their undying loyalty to him in exchange for his largess. By history, Trump was always a Democrat until about the time of the launch of his Birther campaign.[59] (Notably, this was after Trump, by his son's own 2008 account[60], was heavily submerged in Russian money.)

Throughout his life, Trump, a dedicated, malignant narcissist,[61] has had only one true cause - Donald J. Trump. Like his Republican bootlickers, Trump has fed his core constituency the unique goodies they desire and they have given him in return exactly what he craves – unconditional loyalty and the freedom to make a mess of the world.

It sounded ridiculous at the time, but perhaps Trump was outrageously right when he said he could shoot someone on 5th Avenue and he wouldn't lose a single vote from his supporters.[62] Here are some of those one-issue Trump loyalists:

1. Wealthy business interests such as Wall Street, defense contractors, and the fossil fuel industry have cashed in their morality chips for lower taxes and fewer regulations.

Many of these interests have fought for deregulation, tax cuts, and the proliferation of money in politics (corporations are people, money is speech[63]). They have fostered denial of man's role in climate change and lobbied for increasing the military budget, almost always for financial gain. Although unnecessary regulations can be burdensome and wasteful, perhaps the better description of "good" regulations should be "governmental protections." (It is called the Environmental *Protection* Agency.) Hopefully a few examples will make my point.

In 2008 the greatest collapse in the world economy since the Great Depression was brought about in large part by the deregulation of the financial industry and the failure of government institutions in 2006 and 2007 to recognize and respond to the gravity of the impending financial disaster. This policy created an environment in which banks engaged in speculative and fraudulent behaviors.[64] Deregulation of the financial industry (and the resultant greed of banking, investment, and ratings firms) is what caused the collapse, not governmental support for poor families with food stamps and pre-school programs.

Science informs us that man's proliferation of carbon producing activities is warming the planet at an alarming rate. Why have the Chinese, of all governments, come to recognize this fact and seen the advantage in becoming a leading edge in future technologies for alternate fuels,[65] while Trump is championing coal, the 19th Century's favorite energy source? Why are we essentially the only country opposed to the Paris Climate Accord?

What industries will protect our air, water, and soil unless they are required to take appropriate action by the government? If polluting is free of consequences for the offenders, they will continue to offend. We can only clean Los Angeles and Houston's air and West Virginia's rivers with regulations/protections and/or taxes requiring businesses to internalize the external costs (so-called "externalities"[66] such as smog, cancers, heart and lung disease, unsafe water, aesthetics, etc.) of their mining, manufacturing, and trucking enterprises. Trump has given them exactly what they wanted: an incredibly irresponsible, trillion-dollar tax cut (which is primarily beneficial to the rich and large businesses[67]) and a malignant Secretary of the Environmental Protection Agency, Scott Pruit.[68] Pruit's primary departmental goal was the destruction of the very agency he headed. Unbelievably Trump has reversed an Obama era regulation that protected rivers and streams from the toxic, heavy metal pollution dumped by coal companies. The health and environmental risks from this travesty will be felt most profoundly in the communities of Appalachia (ironically a region that was a bedrock of support for Trump).[69]

I have often been frustrated by the failure of Democrats to articulate a message to help America's business class understand that support for programs that help the poor (such as health care, nutrition, pre-school education and family planning) are concurrently beneficial to our wealthy citizens and business interests. Helping as many of the poor rise up to the middle class as possible is an imperative goal; it is in everyone's best interests. Seventy percent of our gross domestic product is driven by *consumption.*[70] Business needs consumers. Business needs skilled workers for the 21st Century economy.

We need a flourishing middle class for more than just economic reasons. A strong argument can be made that a robust middle class helps assure political stability - a thriving democracy. Just ask Aristotle who shared these thoughts about 2400 years ago:

> The best constitution is one controlled by a
> numerous middle class which stands
> between the rich and the poor. For those
> who possess the goods of fortune in
> moderation find it 'easiest to obey the rule
> of reason'. . . . They are accordingly less
> apt than the rich or the poor to act unjustly
> toward their fellow citizens.[71]

2. Ironically the Religious Right has made a pact with the devil.

Although I understand that people of good conscience may, for religious and other reasons, be opposed to a woman's right to choose to have an abortion, I have never understood why such people would align themselves with a political party that fails to show compassion for human beings *after* they are born.[72] Where is the internal consistency in opposing health care, food stamps, and pre-school programs for everyone, especially the poor; programs that help reduce teen and other unwanted-pregnancies, that help promote a healthy, educated, and viable middle class? The Republicans are the party that will tell us we don't have enough money for these and similar essential programs and at the same time give themselves reckless tax cuts and push for further deregulation of the banks, possibly ushering in another financial collapse. How do many of these devout people align themselves with a government that would separate children from their parents who brought their families to America desperately seeking safety and asylum from dangerous, criminal Central American gangs?[73]

There are certainly millions of religious Americans who do not support Trump's immoral offerings. Jonathan Wilson Hartgrove's new book, *Reconstructing The Gospel,* argues that the teachings of the gospel have been manipulated over the centuries by politicians and clergy eager to abridge interpretations of the bible to rationalize immoral behaviors, such as slavery, that Jesus would have abhorred and scorned.[74] I don't intend to be monolithic in my observations about the Religious Right. However, there is no question regarding the strength of support Trump has garnered from the Evangelical Movement.[75]

The point here is that somehow Trump, with the aid of the Republican Party, has found a constituency that will sacrifice many of their religious and moral beliefs for the sake of one or two issues, typically abortion and homosexuality. It seems they may even be willing to sacrifice the very foundations of our democracy, a form of government based on the rule of law, not men, in exchange for the munificence of their dear leader. What would Jesus do?

Based on the premise that the exercise of religion is a celebrated freedom, separate and apart from the administration of government, we recognize the First Amendment as the cornerstone of religious liberty. What we often fail to quote from the amendment's language is the mandate that there shall be no law "respecting an *establishment* of religion".[76] In other words, the government should not be in the business of passing laws promoting one religion or religious idea over another. Tell that to the "Christian Nationalists" who in the guise of "religious freedom" seek to impose Christianity on all of America.[77] Our Founding Fathers included the Establishment Clause in the First Amendment in order to prohibit just such a practice. Certainly they had a concurrent view of religious tolerance also embodied in the First Amendment. I enjoy the observations of Thomas Jefferson who is quoted, noting:

> (I)t does me no injury for my neighbor to believe in twenty gods or no God. It neither picks my pocket nor breaks my leg.[78]

3. *Apparently, the only amendment to the Constitution that truly counts is . . . the Second Amendment.*

There is perhaps no more obvious one-issue group than the gun lobby epitomized by the National Rifle Association. Even though a *majority* of gun rights advocates and gun owners (*including* NRA members) disagree with many of the NRA positions,[79] the

NRA consistently holds serve when it comes to controlling the votes of Congress and the designs of Trump. The NRA is primarily serving the interests of the weapons manufacturers. History shows us that this was not always the case.[80] The propaganda fostered by the gun lobby and their dutiful servants (the Republican Congress and Trump) relies upon misleading and simplistic arguments.

Here's something easy to understand. It's simple *common sense*. (Remember those two words?) The United States has *by far* the highest rate of gun violence in the world. The United States also has *by far* more guns per capita than any country on the planet.[81] The NRA would have us believe that having even *more* guns is the answer to our national epidemic of gun violence.

The NRA's role in the 2016 election may well be linked to the Russian meddling campaign aimed at electing Donald Trump. Recently the Justice Department indicted a Russian gun-rights activist, Maria Butina, linked to the NRA and accused of being a Russian agent.[82] In what would be hard to describe as coincidental, Butina was called upon at one of the first Trump rallies in 2015 to ask Trump a question about Russian sanctions.[83] (He immediately provided a lengthy answer favorable to Putin and in which Trump stated he didn't think we needed to continue the Russian sanctions.) In addition to Butina's federal indictment there are reports of a concurrent investigation into whether the NRA illegally funneled Russian money to the Trump campaign.[84] Putin's apparent support for the NRA was entirely consistent with his ultimate goal to elect Trump and to weaken our country both domestically and internationally. What better way was there to accomplish his aims than to stoke fear and heighten partisan differences by exacerbating the already toxically divided gun control debate?

> **4. *After almost four hundred years of slavery, Jim Crow, and institutional-segregation, as well as African American unemployment persisting at almost 80% higher than white unemployment in the United States,[85] it's obvious that the true victims of racism in the United States . . . are white males.[86]***

The role race has played in Trump's strategic plan has been complex, insidious, and dangerous. While he has frighteningly appealed to the most blatant groups of violent racists,[87] he has furthered his broader strategy by pandering to fearful whites, particularly white males (Steve Schmidt's "victim class"), some of whom believe that their economic and social decline/stagnation was the fault of the growing minority populations (Schmidt's "scapegoats" *singularly* blamed for complex problems). The issues of income inequality and wage stagnation among unskilled workers are probably most affected by globalization, automation, and the squeeze in this country of the social safety net that helps sustain lower income families and provide them a better opportunity to rise up to the middle class.[88] Reasonable people can differ on the weight of all these influences.[89]

We cannot rationally disagree on the nefarious reasons for Trump's cruel, manipulative appeal to the underbelly of prejudice in our country. His aim is to divide America through fear, lies, and hatred. (Have we forgotten Franklin Roosevelt's compelling declaration, echoed by John F. Kennedy, "We have nothing to fear but fear itself"[90]?) In the process, Trump has given license to a worrisome number of individuals to openly express their previously hidden hatreds and racist fears.[91] This fear mongering is clearly the most dangerous weapon in Trump's autocratic arsenal. It violently tears at the fabric of our American society and democracy.

We cannot and should not ignore Trump's blatantly racist manipulations. The list of his cruel comments in the aftermath of Charlottesville (referenced earlier) is only one obvious example. His leadership of the Birther Movement was an insidious, racist, dog whistle aimed at garnering favor with the part of the electorate who were unable to accept the idea of an American *black* President. Trump's techniques are often implied and crafty. Trump's methodology is an attempt to provide political cover all the while sending a clear, sinister message to the racist wing of his base.

There are scores of examples of Trump's race baiting over the course of his lifetime.[92] Prominent African American figures, politicians, newsmen, and sports heroes have been among Trump's favorite targets for abusive, racist rhetoric. He loves demeaning black athletes who have kneeled during NFL games to bring attention to their concern with police violence against minorities. More obviously, Trump has called a number of famous African Americans "low I.Q." or words to that effect. Most recently he said this about basketball star LeBron James:

> Lebron James was just interviewed by the
> dumbest man on television, Don Lemon. He

made Lebron look smart, which isn't easy to do.[93]

Don Lemon happens to be black as well. It is unconscionable for anyone to support a man of Trump's failed moral character to be President of the United States, let alone a local dog catcher.

5. *Trump's message to white, non-college-educated men, who feel powerless and disaffected, explains the core of his support.*[94]

Among the other Trump supporters, perhaps the largest group is comprised of disaffected, non-college-educated, white males. By any electoral standard, membership in this group was the best predictor of a vote for Trump. An article in *The Atlantic* written in March of 2016 during the campaign when it was clear that Trump was prevailing within the Republican primaries was very informative on Trump's appeal to this group.[95] Oddly, during the election campaign many pundits and reporters observed substantial similarities between the positions of Trump and Bernie Sanders.[96] Although I differed personally with some of "Bernie's" positions (I thought TPP was a crucial trade pact firmly establishing our influence in far Pacific trade) I trust that his stated political positions were represented in the best of faith. Trump on the other hand, a shameless liar, sold this interest group (non-college-educated whites) what they wanted to hear. His "policies" were cobbled from a workbench covered in destructive, chaotic, and impulsive notions. His withdrawal from TPP will allow China to fill the American trading void in the Far East. During his campaign, Trump suggested he might support a single-payer health program. He also touted that his health insurance program would be cheaper and cover more people than Obamacare. He promised it would cover everyone.[97] So far all he has done from the Oval Office is undermine some of the key, protective provisions of the Affordable Care Act . . . and provide no alternative. Instead of raising the taxes on the very rich, as he promised, he has given them a trillion-dollar windfall. You get the idea.

6. Republican politicians have one issue – maintain power.

More than anyone else, Republican Congressmen have been willing to sell their integrity and long-standing historic values for the singular sake of staying in power. Here are a few obvious examples.

Republicans have always been ardent defenders of American freedoms as the counterbalance to totalitarianism, most particularly the menace of Soviet Russia. Remember Republican President Ronald Reagan's passionate call (so often quoted fondly by adoring Reaganites), "Mr. Gorbachev, tear down this wall"? Remarkably, they have now been silent for the most part about Trump's embrace of Vladimir Putin and other despots. The only Republican politicians who appear willing in any way to challenge Trump's pathetic patronage of Putin are those Congressmen not seeking reelection.

Republicans are generally free-trade advocates. Trump on the other hand is aggressively advancing a dangerous trade war with most of our major, traditional trading partners. His impulsive, destructive, flailing tariff "policy" has already done serious damage that may have long-term consequences for American farmers.[98] Congress has the power to stop Trump's trade meddling, yet it has been unwilling to take any action thus far.[99] Most of these politicians understand the estimation of historians' and economists' that the passage of the Smoot-Hawley Act, imposing protectionist tariffs in the 1930's, was a major force in causing the disastrous depth of the Great Depression.[100]

Trump's response to the needless crises *he created* in the soybean market was to offer what amounts to a twelve-billion dollar bribe to farmers, to try to mitigate the impact of his reckless behaviors – just ahead of the midterm elections.[101] It reminds me of the Alexi de Tocqueville 19th Century quote I cited earlier from *Democracy in America*, "The American Republic will endure until the day Congress discovers that it can bribe the public with the public's money." Only in this case it is the President attempting to beguile the farmers with their own money.

I have one last example of the Republican sellout. Republicans have traditionally been the party of "family values."[102] Trump is a twice divorced, admitted compulsive adulterer, who was willing to maliciously separate parents from their children for the "crime" of coming to America for the safety of their families. Is this the conduct of a role model for the American family or the moral leader of our country?

In late 2017 Trump's and the Republican Party's endorsement of Alabama's U.S. Senate candidate, Roy Moore, was one of the ugliest examples of Republican political, hypocrisy. At least nine women credibly accused Moore of sexual misconduct occurring when they were teenagers and he was in his thirties.[103] The best Trump could muster when confronted with the multiple allegations against Moore was to state, "Look, he denies it. He denies it."[104] Sound familiar? This was Trump's rationale (quoted earlier at the Trump/Putin Helsinki summit) for supporting Putin's claim that Russia did not meddle in the 2016 elections. "I have President Putin, he just said it's not Russia." [105]

Innocent Complicity

As summarized above, many single-interest groups have been prepared to drink Trump's Kool Aid and/or pretend to look away from his awful words and deeds, often in the service of their greedy personal desires. However, whether we voted for Trump or not, many of us have been in some way complicit in his gaudy, regretful charade. Here are some of the groups of our society who have inadvertently fostered the rise of Trump:

1. An ill-informed public confused by misinformation, lies, and propaganda is easily misled by Trump's snake-oil sales pitch.

Our democracy is suffering from the erosion of public education in civics, history, and current affairs. Add to that the concurrent rise of Internet algorithms designed to reinforce our existing bias (whether well-founded or not) and the malicious mischief of Internet trolls, domestic and foreign, aimed at misleading, confusing, and manipulating public opinion, and we have a messy brew: a breeding ground for con men, conspiracy theorists, and political swindlers to ply their dirty tricks.

I am a reasonably well-informed citizen who grew up schooled in basic government and history. I took it for granted that public schools regularly taught classes in government and civics, teaching us the basic elements of democracy: the balancing effect of our three branches of government; the first amendment protections of a free and independent press; the maxim that we are a country of laws, not men; the equity of "one man, one vote";[106] "the rights of the minority and the rule of the majority".[107] I saw in America what George H.W. Bush described (citing Ronald Reagan citing other sources) as " . . . a shining city upon a hill whose beacon light guides freedom-loving people everywhere."

Never did I anticipate the erosion of public knowledge of basic facts regarding the foundations of our republic. The alarming loss of a basic education in the indispensable foundations of our system of laws may well be delightful comic fodder for late night television.[108] However, it is disturbingly dangerous, particularly when the void in public education is filled by fabrications and lies fed by shock radio jocks,[109] Fox News,[110] Sinclair Broadcast Group,[111] conspiracy mongers,[112] Internet trolls,[113] and a President who is a pathological liar.[114] (I will refer to these purveyors of pernicious falsehoods collectively as the "Echo Chamber.") Like fast food scientifically designed to be consumed in large quantities without chewing, we have been fed stories that are readily digested to satisfy our predisposed tastes, prejudices, and misconceptions. Like a cheeseburger and fries these fabrications and fictions clog our brains with a form of cerebral cholesterol blocking critical thinking, common sense, facts and reason.

"Echo Chamber" is an apt description as each member of the chamber orchestrates the same talking points that he/she harmonizes daily, incessantly, and gleefully, to the listening public.[115]

Each of us has an obligation to be informed. Ignorance is not generally an excuse for abetting con men and despots. Nonetheless one can understand how people of good conscience have been misled to vote and act (often in ways directly against their best interests) due to the insidiously effective false narratives propagated by the Echo Chamber.

2. Trump's most ardent opponents often let the perceived perfect be the enemy of the good. How progressive voters' and politicians' purity has undermined their movement.

We do not have to go too far back in history to draw a direct line between liberal idealism and the several calamities identified with the George W. Bush Presidency. Ralph Nader was the angel of the progressive movement. He ran a third party presidential campaign in 2000 on the premise that there was no difference between the Democrats and Republicans. (This is an appealing message to those who feel powerless in our country and, in a way, correlates with Trump's appeal to "drain the swamp.") Unfortunately, in the 2000 Presidential election 97,488 Florida voters cast their ballot for Nader, throwing the election to George W. Bush who "won" by 537 votes.[116] As for Nader's premise that there was really no difference between voting Republican and Democratic, here are a few notable facts:

- Bush appointed two conservative judges whose rulings have had profound consequences.[117]

- The Bush administration lied to the American public about non-existent "weapons of mass destruction" and led us into a war and occupation that many experts have called the worst foreign policy and military disaster in our history.[118]

- The Bush Supreme Court decision in the case of Citizens United has branded money and corporate influence into the American election process for decades to come, undermining our democracy and the rights of common citizens.[119]

- The Bush Supreme Court gutted the Voting Rights Act.[120]

While I am certain Al Gore would have nominated different judges, I'm also fairly sure Al Gore would not have pursued a tragic, destabilizing war in Iraq, a war that was promoted by Republican Neo-Cons headed by Vice President Cheney.[121] I'm also confident that Bush's father, George H. W. Bush, who stopped short of going to Bagdad during the First Gulf War and even wrote about the absence of wisdom in further destabilizing Iraq (the biggest counterbalance to Iran's influence in the Middle East) would not have attacked Saddam Hussein.[122] (Even H. W. Bush's then Secretary of Defense, Dick Cheney (remember him?) was against invading Bagdad.[123])

Like I said, we can draw a straight line between Ralph Nader's campaign and these disastrous outcomes.

Trump's election chances were also improved by the words and deeds of voters and third-party candidates who are politically to the left of the Democratic Party. I'll reference just two examples: actress Susan Sarandon and Green Party presidential candidate Jill Stein. Sarandon (who supported Nader in 2000) famously refused to support Hillary Clinton (after Bernie failed to get the nomination) and threw her support to Jill Stein.[124] I'm not going to expound here about my reservations with the Green Party candidate's "qualifications," nor examine why she appeared with Mike Flynn at a dinner in Moscow with Vladimir Putin.[125] (I just used a technique Trump has famously employed.) I'll just note the following startling statistic. In the three states that narrowly gave the election to Trump (Wisconsin, Michigan, and Pennsylvania) Jill Stein's vote totals *exceeded* Trump's margin of victory.[126]

Historically, the Democrats have had a knack for cannibalizing their own. In 1968 anti-war activists demonstrated in Chicago during the party's politically-scorching summer convention. The Democratic nominee, Hubert Humphrey, was never able to recover from the television images of Cook County police wielding night sticks and tear gas on the rioting demonstrators while brutal

Mayor Daley thugs beat up journalists on the floor of the convention.[127] Most recently New York Senator Kirsten Gillibrand was the first Democratic politician to call for the resignation of Al Franken, the hugely popular and talented Senator from Minnesota. Rather than afford Senator Franken appropriate due process to confront the allegations of "sexual abuse," he was made a sacrificial lamb of the party.[128] Contrast the Democratic response to accusations against Senator Franken with the Republican's answer to the charges against Donald Trump and his pick for Alabama Senator, Roy Moore and you will see how differently the two parties approach the same problem.

I have one final progressive peeve. While advancing such admirable goals as economic fairness, universal healthcare, and human tolerance, progressives have often conveyed the message of *intolerance* to other segments of our society. They often promote a narrative casting business as the enemy. I prefer the strategy that embraces business along with labor and that recognizes the overlapping interests of the haves and have-nots. Why terrify business owners into thinking that their interests and the interests of the disenfranchised are mutually exclusive? Business provides jobs, goods and services. Creating a positive environment for businesses to flourish obviously serves everyone's best interests. What is the political and social value in demonizing any of the major segments of our society in a world that is already dangerously polarized? Fostering a message that is antagonistic to business owners will continue to drive them to charlatans like Trump for fear that progressives will support legislation that is damaging to their economic welfare.

You get the point. In looking for political purity by favoring unelectable candidates, and by dismissing quality candidates based upon litmus tests such as abortion and gun control, by constantly demonizing the "rich," progressives have let their perceived perfect be the enemy of the good. The Russians are well aware of these tendencies. They know their goals will be served by further nurturing the growing polarization of our society. Why do you think Russian trolls and bots played mischief on the Internet fabricating information supporting left leaning candidates like Jill Stein, who opposed Clinton, and rightwing candidates who challenged Trump, such as Ted Cruz and Marco Rubio?

3. Mainstream media, which has for the most part been diligent in analyzing and exposing Trump's follies (perhaps too superfluous a word to describe Trump's often malignant words and actions), has inadvertently, from the moment he declared his candidacy and up until the present time, been feeding the beast.

Hillary Clinton's presidential campaign cost over one billion dollars. That is not unusual in this extraordinary era of multi-year elections underwritten by virtually unlimited funds, often supplied by unknown sources through PACs (Political Action Committees), and virtually unregulated as legitimized by the Supreme Court in its *Citizens United* debacle.[129] (Thank you Ralph Nader and Susan Sarandon.) What is unusual is that Donald Trump spent a little more than *half* of the Clinton Campaign budget.[130] (Thank you Fox News, CNN, MSNBC, NBC, CBS, ABC . . . well, thank you virtually every major television and cable broadcasting network.)

There's an old adage in television news. "If it bleeds it leads." Trump, the carnival barker and snake-oil salesman understands this well. Every day, virtually every hour, during his campaign and during his presidency, Trump has poured blood into the collective press pool in the form of often outlandish, shocking, racist, misogynistic, provocative, and vile speeches and tweets. What has he received in return? Over a billion dollars of free promotional television time. Even MSNBC, a left leaning cable news and opinion outlet, covered *entire* Trump rallies, often pre-empting their regularly scheduled shows. These are profit making news programs that attract advertisers by garnering viewers - more viewers, more advertising dollars. The public is attracted to Trump like watching a three . . . make that a *five* alarm fire.

When are the news networks (I'm not including Fox in this description) going to stop being played and show a social and moral conscience by ceasing to broadcast the daily orgy of Trump's political pornography?

CHAPTER FIVE

What Are the Consequences of Our Selfish and Ignorant Actions Which Support the Most Chaotic and Destructive Presidency in our History?

In case I have not alarmed you enough about the dangers that prowl in Trump's sometimes hidden agenda (yes, he has a plan, or at least his manipulators have plans for him and us) there are two parallel destructive themes that run through his apparent designs. One domestic. One international. Both dramatically undermine our civic and world order. Not much noticed in the first month of the Trump presidency was an interview with one of his top early advisers, Steve Bannon. Bannon coined the phrase "deconstruction of the administrative state."[131] In essence, Bannon has advocated the elimination, or at a minimum the minimization, of the administrative arms of government with one exception: the military and related security apparatus.

In my view, Bannon's vision for the government of the United States forecasts a rather dreadful, dystopian future for our country. His view of the role of our administrative agencies is really not that far afield from Republican policies over the past decades.

"Let's kill the beast!" If we run vast deficits to fund an unwieldy military and irresponsible tax breaks for the rich there won't be enough resources for the other federal institutions: those aimed at protecting the elderly, the disabled, the poor, our health, education, the environment, our financial system, and general public welfare.[132] The Republican Party always had the reputation (fading rapidly over the recent Republican administrations) for being the party of "fiscal conservatism." The hypocrisy of the Republicans passing a trillion-dollar tax cut concurrent with a substantial increase in the military budget should not be lost on anyone.

And Bannon has been successful in orchestrating his symphony of bureaucratic annihilation. For his overture he managed to have Trump appoint two types of individuals to head the non-military departments of government. Trump either appointed Secretaries who were committed to destroying the very departments they were charged with overseeing and/or who were unimaginably unqualified for their positions.[133] If you have the interest just review the resumes of Trump's cabinet members starting with former Secretary of the Environmental Protection Agency Scott Pruitt, Education Secretary Betsy DeVos, and Energy Secretary Rick Perry.

(Remember him? Energy is the department of government Perry wanted to eliminate but couldn't remember in his infamous performance during one of the Presidential Debates.[134])

While, undoubtedly, improved efficiency in the departments of government is a noble aim, the "deconstruction" of these agencies will be nothing short of tragic.

Trump's second parallel destructive goal has played out profoundly in the international sphere for the entire eighteen months of Trump's presidency. He did not take long to get started. He insulted the Australian Prime Minister in the first two weeks of his term.[135] Just weeks later, Trump profoundly and inexplicably slighted German President Angela Merkel by refusing to shake her hand[136] – when she was a *guest* in the White House – in front of international TV press and cameras. In one more humiliating moment, early in his presidency Trump actually *shoved aside* the Prime Minister of Montenegro, the leader of a member country of NATO.[137] When I originally viewed the video of Trump's arrogant shove I was struck by his presumptive, pushy, ugly demeanor. As an American I was embarrassed and dismayed. I was sadly reminded of black and white images of Italy's pompous fascist dictator Benito Mussolini.

As referenced earlier, Trump has continued during his term to insult our closest allies and to disrupt our most important strategic and democratic relationships. What is remarkable is the fact that all of those damaging actions, both domestic and foreign, perfectly coincide with the interests/designs of Vladimir Putin: the disruption of the American economy and political system, the destruction of America's standing in the international community, and the ruin of the unity of the NATO alliance.

In addition to these two terrible consequences of the Trump presidency, I see a plethora of other devastating costs. My purpose in writing this composition does not allow me enough time to delve into all the reasons and rationale for my concerns. Nevertheless, here is a brief summary of some of my greatest apprehensions concerning both Trump's "leadership" as well as the Republican Party's well-worn agenda:

1. *The Destruction of our social contract.*

In pitting one group of Americans against the other, Trump is undermining the very core of our civil society while playing on our fears and prejudices. We have nothing to fear but the fear Trump wants us to embrace.

Daily, sometimes even hourly, Trump has implemented a consistent strategy to tell/sell the same lies and misinformation over and over again, so that his minions will come to believe his "alternate" world reality. "Fake news!" "No collusion!" "Witch hunt!"

I think Joseph Goebbels, Adolf Hitler's infamous Nazi Propaganda Minister, probably best explained the thinking behind Trump's incessant public lying:

> If you tell a lie big enough and keep repeating it, people will eventually come to believe it. The lie can be maintained only for such time as the State can shield the people from the political, economic and/or military consequences of the lie. It thus becomes vitally important for the State to use all of its powers to repress dissent, for the truth is the mortal enemy of the lie, and thus by extension, the truth is the greatest enemy of the State.[138]

Goebbels was reaffirming the often-quoted statement of his dear Führer, Adolf Hitler, "Make the lie big, make it simple, keep saying it, and eventually they will believe it."[139] Trump must be an excellent student. "Fake news!" "No collusion!" "Witch Hunt!" "Russian Hoax!"

Do Goebbels' and Hitler's words send chills down your back? They should. Need I remind you that Trump has repeatedly called the media the "enemy of the American people" sandwiched between one-thousand declarations of "Fake News!", often while pointing his ominous finger at the *real* news cameras lining the back of his blood-stirring rallies.

Do you think the Goebbels and Hitler references are too inflammatory? Trump's ex-wife, Ivana, has claimed that Trump kept copies of Hitler speeches by his bedside. When contacted by Vanity Fair Trump gave a denial that was "less than reassuring."[140]
We do not have to draw a straight line between the most infamous Nazi villians in world history to Donald Trump. His sinister methodology coincides perfectly with the corrupting methods of their madness. The net effect of Trump's repeated lies, misinformation, and hate speech is to tear apart the fabric of America's civil order, to inflame old prejudices and differences, rather than to heal them.

2. *The oppression of minority rule.*

Through aggressive gerrymandering (the manipulation of Congressional district boundaries allowing a minority of voters to control legislative seats) we now have a country in which a minority of the voters is determining the fate of the majority of citizens.[141] In addition to that, Republican legislatures have passed laws aimed at making it more difficult for minorities, the poor, the elderly, and students to vote.[142] Remember the idea of the *rule* of the majority and the rights of the minority?

> ### 3. The accelerated erosion of the environment and the loss of potential jobs and opportunity in leading the 21st Century technological boom in alternative energy.

Coal is not the answer. It is part of the problem. When else in our history has it been a good idea to favor an old, inefficient, outdated technology over a new, superior one? Coal is not only an obsolete technology; it is destructive of our environment and our health.

> ### 4. Further decay of our infrastructure.

The ramifications are profound as our roads, bridges, and electrical grid all continue to age and undermine the life and economy of the United States. When we spend money on infrastructure we are investing in America. Ask anyone to describe the best investment he or she has made in his or her lifetime and the probable answer will be the purchase of a home. Our roads, bridges, and electrical grid are all assets that serve our businesses and the quality of our lives. These are necessary investments that not only provide good paying jobs during their construction but also return economic and aesthetic dividends for decades.[143]

5.   *Healthcare – Need I Say More?*

Trump and the Republicans have done everything in their power to undermine the Affordable Care Act while providing no alternative to the overwhelming problem of healthcare in America. We are the *only* developed nation (out of thirty-three) that does not have a universal health care program.[144] The Affordable Care Act, though flawed, was our first real attempt to address this massive issue. Trump and the Republicans have done everything in their power to fracture the act, even though it was based upon a *conservative* think-tank's vision.[145] I guess the biggest problem with the Affordable Care Act was the fact that our first black president endorsed it. (If that sounds cynical, it is intended to be. The Republican Party's unrelenting attack on President Obama, beginning with the Birther Movement, was an unapologetic, thinly disguised racial assault. Remember Newt Gingrich's (and more recently Rudolf Giuliani's) reference to Obama's "Kenyan, anti-colonial behavior"?[146]

6. Disruption of Seventy Years of World Order.

Trump's language and methods have been damaging both domestically and internationally. He has been engaged in a strategy that is threatening seventy years of world stability.

"Make it simple, keep saying it." Trump has consistently followed that formula. His two most ubiquitous mottos are "America First!" and "Make America Great Again." They are emblazoned with white lettering on perhaps millions of red baseball caps.

The reality of Trump's world is the antithesis of those jingoistic declarations. The more accurate slogans should be "America *Last*!" and "Make America *Alone* Again!" Trump is withdrawing America from the world stage, conjuring up memories of the 1930's isolationism, which was driven by the Depression and the residual collective despair over the tragic First World War. Our entry into World War II changed all that, and in the seventy years since we have been a robust leader of world economics, politics, health, the environment, and diplomacy.

Trump has now abandoned the Trans Pacific Partnership, allowing China to fill the void. He has deserted our allies and walked away from the Iran nuclear deal, presumably leaving in its wake uncertainty and the threat of war. He has unilaterally forsaken the Paris Climate Accord while fostering domestic antagonism against new clean energy sources, once again deferring to China to fill the technological vacuum. He has threatened to undermine our leadership of NATO, the most important world defense answer to the military threat of totalitarian regimes. Lives have been lost and entire careers have been spent ensuring the continuity of America's role in the world. Trump is engaged in a mission to destroy that legacy.

On August 6, 2018 Joe Scarborough interviewed Dr. Richard Haass (long-time President of the Council on Foreign Relations) on Scarborough's MSNBC show *Morning Joe.* Dr. Haass is one of the foremost experts in international relations in the country with a resume serving both Republican (including Ronald Reagan) and Democratic presidents.[147] Scarborough asked Dr. Haass what he thought the impact was of Donald Trump's constant lying on America's standing in the world. Here is a portion of what Dr. Haass warned:

> The implications are terrible . . . .
>
> One, is we've got a divided country . . . many people can not believe what their president says. So, how can we act in a unified, concerted, consistent way?
>
> Second of all, some of the most important things the United States does in foreign policy has nothing to do with diplomats or our soldiers. It's the example we set . . . .
>
> This is not quite a shining city on a hill. The idea that we're having the coarseness of this dialogue, this degree of untruths said, this is not a country that the rest of the world will respect.
>
> . . . . We should never forget the rest of the world depends on us. If we are seen as lying, if we are seen as not being reliable, essentially the rest of the world will take its fate into its own hands. . . . This will be a world that will be far less stable . . . .
>
> That won't just be bad for the world . . . . It will come back and it will undermine prosperity and stability and security here at home. This is serious. This is consequential.

6. ***The Loss of Our Moral Compass.***

Trump has infected the public dialogue in this country with hatred, lies, and thinly-veiled racist slurs. At the same time he has created an environment in which people actually debate the "merits" of summarily and cruelly separating small children from their parents because they had the audacity to flee dangerous gangs in Central America. Is this the America we grew up admiring? Really?

Fortunately for us, one prominent American politician has articulated a clear moral standard for the person who holds the highest office in the country. The following quotation establishes a firm rationale for the resignation or impeachment of a president who does not, by his or her own practice, live up to the highest principles of decency:

> If you and I fall into bad moral habits, we
> can harm our families, our employers and
> our friends. The President of the United
> States can incinerate the planet. Seriously,
> the very idea that we ought to have . . .
> less than the same moral
> demands placed on the Chief Executive
> that we place on our next-door neighbor
> is ludicrous and dangerous. Throughout
> our history, we have seen the presidency
> as the repository of all of our highest
> hopes and ideals and values. To demand
> less is to do an injustice to the blood that
> bought our freedoms."[148]

> Further, the President's repeated lies to
> the American people
> . . . compound the case against him as
> they demonstrate his failure to protect the
> institution of the presidency as the
> 'inspiring supreme symbol of all that is
> highest in our American ideals'. Leaders
> affect the lives of families far beyond
> their own 'private life'.[149]

I wrote earlier about the duplicity of the Republican Party's and the Religious Right's unquestioning support for Trump, in violation of many of their long-standing values. Sadly, the above quotes epitomize the magnitude of this hypocrisy. The source of these high-minded quotes is none other than Vice President Mike Pense, one of Trump's foremost lackeys and enablers.

CHAPTER SIX

What We Must and Can Do
Our Moral and Civic Duty

I am truly worried. I have written this work in the hope that it can inspire other people to action who, like me, have taken for granted the constancy of our democracy.[150] Just as the sun dutifully rises in the east and sets in the west I have always assumed that the major foundations of our republic would forever support the essential pillars of democracy. My faith in the stanchions of our republic was never so naïve that I was oblivious to their vulnerability, or that I was unaware of the moments in history when those institutions failed us. It is possible that John F. Kennedy's election to the Presidency in 1960 owed a disturbing debt to Mayor Daily's Chicago machine that allegedly stuffed the Cook County ballot boxes thereby tossing Illinois, and the Presidency, to Kennedy and the Democrats. More recently we should all be aware of the Bush vs. Gore Florida election debacle.

Nevertheless, I always had the belief that our institutions would eventually restore order. Today, with a President who is willing to consistently slander the American press and who is eager to undermine the public's faith in the national, criminal justice system, with a President who is aggressively abetted by a Republican-controlled Congress, I am not so sure . . . not so sure that the foundations of our system of laws and democratic institutions will prevail. Notably, our system of checks and balances has failed to protect us from Trump's offences due to the willingness of the Republican Congress to do the bidding of our Traitor-In-Chief.

Trump's Republican enablers dwell most notably in the House of Representatives. Two Representatives, each with distinctly different styles, epitomize the current, rolling car wreck that is the Republican led Congress. Devon Nunes, Chairman of the House Permanent Select Committee on Intelligence, has conducted himself so horribly that some commentators have described him as "Trump and Putin's most useful idiot on Capitol Hill". [151] John Heilemann, a thoughtful and respected political analyst, has suggested that Nunes may well be a Russian agent, that there is no better explanation but that Nunes has been compromised. [152]

The other Trump Congressman who has quietly but profoundly fostered Trump's mischief is the often-silent Speaker of the House, Paul Ryan.[153] Do not be misled by his boyish countenance. Without Ryan's complicity, characters such as Nunes would have no power. The Speaker of the House appoints the committee chairmen. Fortunately Speaker Ryan is not running for reelection.

Democracy may be fragile. It turns out that it is more vulnerable than I ever imagined. It requires constant engagement and involvement from its citizens. This can be an often frustrating and even disillusioning process, but when well-meaning, thoughtful and compassionate citizens disengage from the process, those who would do it harm will fill the void. Perhaps the greatest enemy of our democracy is the complacency of good people.[154]

It can often feel like our worthy intentions and hard work lead to very little progress in our politics. Such is the nature of democracy.[155] Those who are stubbornly satisfied only with the complete fulfillment of their ideals lose the battles that those willing to compromise can win in the frustratingly slow process of maintaining and improving our society. As I have shared, we are doomed if we allow the perceived perfect to be the enemy of the good. That is why it is our duty to stay informed and engaged, and to continue to fight for what is right and what is fair, despite those frequent times when it feels like we are making no progress at all. Sometimes our responsibility is as much to prevent our society from worsening, as it is to make it better. For all our frustration with the incompetency in Washington, our best interests were hardly served by our country's reactionary response to our governmental malaise by electing a coarse, dishonest, and fear-mongering conman to the highest office in this land, to the most powerful position in the world.

Again, engaging in the national debate can feel frustratingly ineffectual or even futile, when you consider that you are only one person with one voice and one vote. However, if everyone *dis*engaged from the process for that reason, then nothing would ever change. Conversely, when a million people raise their voices together, when a million people march, our government and society must take notice. It may not always lead to immediate and satisfying reform, but it is a start. All progress begins with a single step, often continuing forward by inches rather than miles. Civil rights reform was slow, inconsistent, and deliberate. We continue to deal with the ways in which we seek equality and fairness. Good things happen when we engage, speak up, and get involved.

So, as we look at the current state of our politics and the frightening degree to which our President and others in his camp seek to tear down the fundamentals of our democracy, it is our greater civic and moral duty to check him and challenge them. Perhaps Congress might impeach this President for his treacherous behavior and dangerously un-American ways, but we cannot wait and hope for that to happen. We cannot continue to be spectators. We must join the fight. We must elect government officials, on both a state and federal level, who will begin the process of change. If we want Congress to take action, then *we* must take action. We need to elect new Congressmen and Congresswomen in the midterm elections. So, in this time of great peril, well-meaning, thoughtful, and compassionate citizens, who might normally feel disillusioned by the frustrating inertia of politics, must recognize the fact that if they do their part, they can change the misguided course of our country.

At the very least, every citizen should vote. Registering to vote, getting informed regarding the issues, and showing up at the polls on election day (not just every four years in a presidential election, but in every midterm election: local, state & federal) are the essential things we all can and must do. Beyond that basic and sacred duty, now is a time for a greater commitment - from each of us. When the Congress has failed to challenge the obscenities of our Executive there is no greater safeguard than the conscience of the public, with each person voting, marching, and engaging others to do the same - to fully engage in the struggle. After all it is supposed to be a government of and by the *people*.

I'm reminded of the Hans Christian Anderson tale *The Emperor's New Clothes.*[156] In the story the Emperor hires weavers who happen to be con men. They "weave" the Emperor a new set of royal garments that are invisible and tell the Emperor that the only people who cannot see the clothes are stupid. No one wants to admit that he is stupid, and certainly no one wants to offend the Emperor, so they all applaud and cheer the Emperor and his grand wardrobe. Only a young boy is willing to declare what is obvious to him, and should be obvious to everyone. The Emperor is naked.

The difference in our current political crises is that the Emperor is in fact the con man. He is telling us that the metaphorical robes of his presidency entrust him with great powers and wisdom. He's the *greatest* negotiator.[157] No one knows the system better than Trump. No one is tougher on ISIS. No one is more conservative. No one helps the disabled more. No one builds better walls. No one respects women more. No one fights for equality more. He has actually made all of these preposterous declarations and more.[158] Even a child can see that Trump has clothed his Presidency in a gilded fabric woven of lies, hatred, racism, chaos, destruction, treachery, narcissism, and subversion. The thing speaks for itself.

We must ask ourselves, who among us remains unwilling to see this despicable man for what even a child must readily know? Who in our midst does not see what former Vice President Joe Biden profoundly observed during a recent speech in Phoenix, Arizona:

> We're in the midst of an all-out assault on
> human dignity. . . . [G]rotesque lies about
> immigrants and policies that rip babies from
> their mothers' arms carry echoes of the
> darkest moments in our history. . . . Not only
> are they a national shame, they tarnish the
> very idea of America and diminish our
> standing in the world.

We all need to join the fight. There is no telling what mischief Trump and his allies (yes, I'm including Vladimir Putin and his Internet arsonists) will spawn in the lead up to the midterm elections. Anything is possible. Lies and misinformation will dominate the Internet and campaign ads. Trump will stoke fears of everything imaginable. He will continue to berate the press and our national justice and security apparatus in his growing attack on our democracy. At rallies, on Twitter, and through surrogates such as Fox News, he will continue to incite his base to hatred, fear, and intolerance. He will embrace conspiracy theories. He will engage in race bating. He will exploit our distrust of Iran and beat the drums of war. He will take credit for everything good and blame President Obama and Hillary Clinton for everything bad.

It is time to make America good again, and we all must play a role. Here's what we can and must urgently do.

There are two obvious ways we can help. We can give of our time and/or our money. My emphasis here is on volunteering. Not everyone can afford to contribute hard-earned dollars. However, to the extent that we are financially able, giving strategic donations of *any* amount is helpful. I recommend giving both to specific organizations such as the Democratic Party (both the National and State organizations) as well as to Democratic candidates in key Congressional and Senate races, as well as to local and state campaigns.

Volunteering should start *now* with only three short months to the midterms. Some of us may be intimidated by the thought of working for a political campaign. There are jobs for everyone regardless of one's talent or temperament. If you are a shy introvert there is definitely a job for you. A great deal of campaign work can be ministerial and uneventful. Volunteers do not have to be fluent in political issues, nor do they have to worry about confronting voters in debates about the candidates. Much of the work is aimed at getting people registered to vote, voting by absentee ballot, and to the polls on Election Day.

If you live in a district where your representative or Senator has an insurmountable lead you can always volunteer in other jurisdictions for one or more other campaigns, whether they are within commuting distance or are more remote. A great deal of work can be done by phone and/or via the Internet.

And of course you can provide additional support through other means mentioned earlier in this work. You should march when there is such an event to attend. Also, phoning and emailing your representatives is a truly meaningful pursuit. Notwithstanding that we all carry the burden of well-earned cynicism regarding our current political environment, generally politicians are susceptible to voters' opinions and the number of phone calls and emails received can be impactful.

Here are a number of important links for engaging you in volunteering and/or donating:

Chop Wood, Carry Water. Here is a good starting point to sign up for daily actions that will take only five minutes:

Democratic National Campaign. This is a terrific general resource for volunteering.

https://my.democrats.org/page/s/help-elect-democrats

Association of State Democratic Committees. This is a more proximate resource for making local contact.

https://asdc.democrats.org/state-parties/

Brand New Congress. Here's a site that is geared toward garnering volunteers to get out the vote and raise funds.

https://brandnewcongress.org

Swing Left. This is a terrific site dedicated to taking back the House of Representatives by targeting the closest races.

https://swingleft.org/about

Here is the Swing Left sign up page.

https://swingleft.org/join?v=p&source=sl-lb-

volrec0618search_house_hlc16d2&gclid=EAIaIQobChMIsP

2n7ZHH3AIVCHZeCh3fEQlXEAAYASAAEgIO-_D_BwE

Nine House Races That Could Flip. This link has nine races in which the Democratic candidates can definitely use your help. https://www.vox.com/2018/6/4/17390070/california-primary-2018-midterms-house-blue-wave

Here are the 9 Democratic candidates and their districts:

10th District – Josh Harder –

https://www.harderforcongress.com

22nd District – Andrew Janz –

http://www.andrewjanzforcongress.org A former prosecutor, Andrew is running against Devon Nunes whose actions as chairman of the House Permanent Select Committee on Intelligence have been malignant at best. If you are going to volunteer for anyone, supporting Andrew Janz is a *necessity*. Here's his website again:

http://www.andrewjanzforcongress.org

25th District – Katie Hill – https://katiehillforcongress.com

39th District – Gil Cisneros –

https://cisnerosforcongress.com

45th District – Katie Porter – https://katieproter.com

48th District – Harley Rouda –

https://harleyforcongress.com Harley is another candidate

you should *eagerly* support. He's running in Orange County

California against Dana Rohrabacher, a fanatical Trump

supporter with worrisome ties to Russia cited here:

https://www.mercurynews.com/2018/07/18/orange-county-

congressman-rohrabacher-met-with-accused-spy-in-russia/

And here: http://www.latimes.com/politics/la-pol-

rohrabacher-russia-timeline-20170804-htmlstory.html

49th District – Mike Levin – https://mikelevin.org

50th District – Ammar Campa-Najjar –

https://www.campacampaign.com

Other ways you can help. Check these out. They are great resources.

The Last Weekend. https://thelastweekend.org This is a big deal. It's a website dedicated to mobilizing volunteers around the nation to get the vote out in the last four days before the midterms. It's an aggregation of 22 progressive groups led by Swing Left.

March On - https://www.wearemarchon.org

March For Our Lives - https://marchforourlives.com This is the Parkland Students' inspired site that is aimed at sensible gun control through marching/demonstrating and getting out the vote.

MoveOn.org - https://front.moveon.org

Mobilize America - https://events.mobilizeamerica.io

Indivisible - https://www.indivisible.org

Flippable - https://flippable.org

Fifteen Ways to Help a Campaign Win -

https://politicalcharge.org/2018/05/04/15-ways-to-help-a-campaign-win-their-election/

The Progressive Turnout Project -

https://www.turnoutpac.org

Democratic Attorneys General Association –

https://democraticags.org

And Finally . . .

There is no way to overstate the dangers that exist today for our democracy. Sadly, the prognostications of George Orwell from his dystopian, savage, satirical novel, *1984,* give us a tragically bleak perspective on the notion of power:

> We know that no one ever seizes power with the intention of relinquishing it. Power is not a means; it is an end. One does not establish a dictatorship in order to safeguard a revolution; one makes the revolution in order to establish the dictatorship. The object of persecution is persecution. The object of torture is torture. The object of power is power. Now you begin to understand me.[159]

And yet, the idealist in me requires that I end on a hopeful note. As I sat in the 1960's in my high-school-government class I was inspired by a brilliant teacher who painted a pragmatic but glorious view of the wonderful possibilities of our government (though admittedly flawed) that George Washington once termed, " . . . the last great experiment for promoting human happiness."[160]

Trump and his cohorts engaged in a concerted effort to demean and defame America's first black president. President Obama, imperfect as he and all presidents have been, was and is intelligent, thoughtful, respectful, disciplined, empathetic, and honest. Trump, Fox News, the NRA, and much of the Republican Party spent a decade trying to vilify President Obama. Although they could not change the reality of the character of that fine, self-made man, they *were* able to alter their constituents' perception of Obama. However, we must not allow those malicious untruths to tarnish the luster of Trump's predecessor's inspiring, good words and deeds.

It is with the truth of President Obama's story in mind that I share two of his quotes to remind all of us where the power lies to effect the change we want, starting with the coming midterms in November.

Change will not come if we wait for some other person or some other time. We are the ones we've been waiting for. We are the change that we seek.[161]

And . . .

One voice can change a room. And if one voice can change a room, then it can change a city. And if it can change a city, it can change a state. And if it can change a state, it can change a nation, and if it can change a nation, it can change the world. Your voice can change the world.[162]

Let's get to work.

References

---

[1] Pledge of Allegiance

[2] http://checkyourfact.com/2018/06/20/fact-check-asylum-seekers-illegal-entry/

[3] https://en.wikipedia.org/wiki/The_Eternal_Jew_%281940_film%29

[4] https://en.wikipedia.org/wiki/1790_United_States_Census

[5] President William Jefferson Clinton's First Inaugural Address January 20, 1993

[6] Spoken at a meeting of the Riverside County Young Republicans in Murrieta, California in August of 2017.

[7] http://www.cnn.com/2002/ALLPOLITICS/02/28/nixon.tapes/

[8] https://www.washingtonpost.com/news/opinions/wp/2016/11/28/trump-just-proved-hes-a-pathological-liar-which-part-is-worse-the-lying-or-the-pathology/?noredirect=on&utm_term=.b7ceb653a05e

[9] Occam's Razor is a principle that suggests the following: "Suppose there exist two explanations for an occurrence. In this case the simple one is usually better." https://simple.wikipedia.org/wiki/Occam%27s_razor

[10] Res Ipsa Loquitor   "…a doctrine that infers negligence from the very nature of an accident or injury in the absence of direct evidence on how any defendant behaved… the elements of duty of care, breach and causation are inferred from an injury that does not ordinarily occur without negligence." See https://en.wikipedia.org/wiki/Res_ipsa_loquitur

[11] https://images.search.yahoo.com/search/images?p=trump+un+photos+with+flags+behind&fr=aaplw&imgurl=https%3A%2F%2Fwww.thenation.com%2Fwp-content%2Fuploads%2F2018%2F06%2FTrump-Kim-handshake-rtr-img.jpg#id=1&iurl=https%3A%2F%2Fwww.thenation.com%2Fwp-content%2Fuploads%2F2018%2F06%2FTrump-Kim-handshake-rtr-img.jpg&action=click

[12] What Bill Maher has alarmingly termed "a slow moving coup"

[13] Trump, D. J. (2017, Feb 5). Bill O'Reilly's Super Bowl Interview with President Trump. (B. O'Reilly, Interviewer). Retrieved from http://video.foxnews.com/v/5311416183001/?#sp=show-clips. Transcript: https://www.sbnation.com/2017/2/5/14516156/donald-trump-interview-transcript-bill-oreilly-super-bowl-2017

[14] http://www.latimes.com/politics/la-na-pol-trump-nato-20180712-story.html

[15] https://www.theguardian.com/us-news/2018/jul/15/donald-trump-vladimir-putin-helsinki-russia-indictments

[16] https://www.nbcnews.com/news/us-news/intelligence-director-says-agencies-agree-russian-meddling-n785481

[17] https://www.politico.com/story/2018/07/16/trump-russia-putin-summit-722418

[18] https://www.presidentsusa.net/oathofoffice.html

[19] https://www.politico.com/story/2018/07/16/trump-russia-putin-summit-722418

[20] Nazi German - https://www.ushmm.org/outreach/en/article.php?ModuleId=10007677; Soviet Union - https://en.wikipedia.org/wiki/Censorship_in_the_Soviet_Union; Russia today - https://www.theguardian.com/commentisfree/2017/mar/24/putin-russia-media-state-government-control; Turkey today - https://en.wikipedia.org/wiki/Censorship_in_Turkey

[21] http://www.nydailynews.com/news/politics/president-trump-labels-news-media-enemy-american-people-article-1.2975293

[22] https://www.huffingtonpost.com/entry/trump-jail-journalists-james-comey-memos_us_5ad96befe4b029ebe0229019

[23] https://en.wikipedia.org/wiki/Anti-intellectualism

[24] http://www.latimes.com/politics/la-na-pol-trump-elites-20170725-story.html#

[25] https://en.wikipedia.org/wiki/Anti-intellectualism

[26] http://www.latimes.com/politics/la-na-pol-trump-elites-20170725-story.html#

[27] See *How Democracies Die* by Steve Levitsky and Daniel Ziblatt

[28] Democracy alert. *Every* seat in the House of Representatives is up for election this fall.

[29] Undisputed by any of our federal governmental investigatory agencies (e.g. F.B.I, C.I.A, D.H.S., etc.) but questioned to this day by our President, the subject of this investigation into the possibility of collusion with Russia within the Trump campaign. If he quacks like a duck . . . .

[30] Trump and his minions have been attacking the credibility of this decorated war hero when paradoxically Trump shrewdly avoided the draft. https://www.nytimes.com/2016/08/02/us/politics/donald-trump-draft-record.html

[31] https://en.wikipedia.org/wiki/Robert_Mueller

[32] https://www.politico.com/story/2016/08/donald-trump-rigged-election-226588

[33] See *How Democracies Die* by Steve Levitsky and Daniel Ziblatt

[34] http://www.nydailynews.com/news/politics/trump-outrageous-comments-mexicans-article-1.2773214

[35] https://www.youtube.com/watch?v=K627iWlbLhY

[36] http://www.latimes.com/politics/washington/la-na-essential-washington-updates-republicans-in-congress-re-up-their-1502835025-htmlstory.html

[37] (See https://www.youtube.com/watch?v=WIs2L2nUL-0)

[38] https://www.bostonglobe.com/opinion/editorials/2017/05/19/trump-shameful-silence-turkish-protest/NbEg9SkMXZYUtefz0cYYcK/story.html

[39] https://en.wikipedia.org/wiki/Steve_Schmidt

[40] *Schmidt Chris Hayes June 26, 2018.https://www.youtube.com/watch?v=FtoNGTmCgvM; See also* https://www.msnbc.com/deadline-white-house/watch/steve-schmidt-trump-s-doj-attacks-the-hallmark-of-autocratic-leadership-1241425987893

[41] Actually the "defendant" in a civil action who may be "accused" of civil wrong doing.

[42] Say for example one has a surgery and days later a fever develops.   The patient has tests that show that there is a surgical sponge in the patient's belly. In this case the burden shifts to the hospital/surgeon to prove that they were *not* responsible for the mistake.

[43] https://www.vox.com/2018/3/1/17062036/trump-russia-midterm-election-2018

[44] http://www.newsweek.com/2017/12/29/donald-trump-russia-secret-deutsche-bank-753780.html

[45] https://www.businessinsider.com/donald-trump-jr-said-money-pouring-in-from-russia-2018-2

[46] https://www.washingtonpost.com/opinions/trump-breaks-his-tax-returns-promise--for-the-third-year-in-a-row/2018/04/16/581552a8-3f3c-11e8-a7d1-e4efec6389f0_story.html?utm_term=.f8567e05af10

[47] https://medium.com/@KeithDB/a-running-tab-of-mueller-investigation-convictions-indictments-f518b9a72827

[48] https://www.nytimes.com/2017/11/14/us/politics/sessions-russia-trump-putin-judiciary-hearing.html

[49] https://themoscowproject.org/explainers/trumps-russia-cover-up-by-the-numbers-70-contacts-with-russia-linked-operatives/

[50] http://www.latimes.com/politics/washington/la-na-essential-washington-updates-trump-s-statements-linking-russia-1494682462-htmlstory.html

[51] https://www.theatlantic.com/magazine/archive/2018/03/paul-manafort-american-hustler/550925/

[52] https://www.politico.com/story/2016/12/trump-drain-swamp-promise-232938

[53] https://www.marketplace.org/2018/02/16/world/ethics-be-damned-more-half-trumps-20-

person-cabinet-has-engaged-questionable-or

[54] https://www.quora.com/Who-has-a-larger-GDP-California-or-Russia

[55] https://www.forbes.com/sites/johnmauldin/2016/12/27/low-oil-prices-will-make-russia-more-aggressive-in-2017/#5faff3017367

[56] https://www.zmescience.com/science/clean-coal-lie-13072017/

[57] https://www.vox.com/policy-and-politics/2017/10/18/16495288/trump-responsibility Trump was tutored by Roy Cohn, attorney to the notorious Senator Joe McCarthy who led a wicked Communist witchhunt in the 1950's. Trump has never forgotten Cohn's motto. Always attack, never apologize. https://www.politico.com/magazine/story/2016/04/donald-trump-roy-cohn-mentor-joseph-mccarthy-213799

[58] "The American Republic will endure until the day Congress discovers that it can bribe the public with the public's money." *Democracy in America,* Alexis de Tocqueville

[59] https://www.npr.org/sections/itsallpolitics/2015/07/28/426888268/donald-trumps-flipping-political-donations

[60] https://www.businessinsider.com/donald-trump-jr-said-money-pouring-in-from-russia-2018-2

[61] While it is difficult to make a psychological diagnosis of people from afar, and admittedly I have no expertise in psychiatry, a number of well-qualified doctors have hypothesized Trump's more than apparent personality disorder. https://www.theatlantic.com/health/archive/2016/07/trump-and-sociopathy/491966/

[62] https://twitter.com/i/moments/691002685949100032?ref_src=twsrc%5Eappleosx%7Ctwcamp%5Esafari%7Ctwgr%5Esearch

[63] https://billmoyers.com/2015/01/21/five-years-citizens-united/; https://www.huffingtonpost.com/chris-weigant/hidden-dangers-of-emcitiz_b_454396.html

[64] https://www.nytimes.com/2011/01/26/business/economy/26inquiry.html

[65] https://www.theguardian.com/environment/2017/jan/06/china-cementing-global-dominance-of-renewable-energy-and-technology

[66] https://en.wikipedia.org/wiki/Externality

[67] https://www.washingtonpost.com/news/wonk/wp/2017/09/28/9-ways-trumps-tax-plan-is-a-gift-to-the-rich-including-himself/?utm_term=.2238b2a3e486 - The tax cut will undoubtedly starve the federal government of funding drastically needed for public infrastructure projects.

[68] Pruit recently resigned. https://en.wikipedia.org/wiki/Scott_Pruitt

[69] https://www.nrdc.org/trump-watch/trump-signs-repeal-drinking-water-protection-measure; see also https://www.onegreenplanet.org/news/governments-decision-to-allow-coal-debris-dumping-in-streams/

[70] https://www.thebalance.com/components-of-gdp-explanation-formula-and-chart-3306015

[71] https://underground.net/aristotle-and-the-middle-class/

[72] I'm further perplexed by the Religious Right's rationale behind opposing contraception, a tool that undoubtedly profoundly lowers the rate of unwanted pregnancies. https://www.psychologytoday.com/us/blog/sexual-intelligence/201706/why-does-the-religious-right-hate-your-birth-control

[73] Ironically one of the primary causes of the rise of gangs in Central America, and the resultant rise of immigrants seeking asylum in the United States, is our policy of deporting violent, convicts to nations such as Honduras, El Salvador and Guatemala. http://www.slate.com/blogs/the_slatest/2017/02/23/deporting_criminals_to_central_america_helped_cause_the_same_violence_that.html

[74] https://asistasjourney.com/2018/06/05/book-review-reconstructing-the-gospel/

[75] http://www.chicagotribune.com/news/opinion/commentary/ct-trump-evangelicals-

support-20171006-story.html
[76] https://www.usconstitution.net/xconst_Am1.html
[77] https://www.theguardian.com/world/2018/jun/04/project-blitz-the-legislative-assault-by-christian-nationalists-to-reshape-america
[78] https://www.cnn.com/2015/07/02/living/america-christian-nation/index.html
[79] http://time.com/5197807/stricter-gun-laws-nra/
[80] https://www.huffingtonpost.com/entry/opinion-young-nra-history_us_5a907fbee4b03b55731c2169
[81] https://en.wikipedia.org/wiki/Estimated_number_of_guns_per_capita_by_country
[82] https://abcnews.go.com/Politics/russian-gun-rights-activist-linked-nra-indicted-acting/story?id=56649422
[83] https://heavy.com/news/2018/07/maria-butina-donald-trump-video-2015/
[84] https://www.snopes.com/news/2018/02/16/did-kremlin-give-money-to-nra/
[85] https://www.bls.gov/web/empsit/cpsee_e16.htm
[86] https://www.npr.org/2017/10/24/559604836/majority-of-white-americans-think-theyre-discriminated-against; https://www.theatlantic.com/science/archive/2017/08/the-worlds-worst-support-group/536850/
[87] http://www.slate.com/blogs/the_slatest/2017/08/14/donald_trump_s_ties_to_alt_right_white_supremacists_are_extensive.html
[88] There is no question that non-college educated whites, particularly white males, have suffered economically during the recent past decades. See e.g. https://www.theatlantic.com/politics/archive/2016/03/who-are-donald-trumps-supporters-really/471714/ ; Trump has successfully played upon this group's fear, dismay and economic erosion by falsely scapegoating minorities and immigrants as the cause of this group's plight.
[89] See for example this quote from economist Paul Krugman from January 2015, "Competition from emerging-economy exports has surely been a factor depressing wages in wealthier nations, although probably not the dominant force. More important, soaring incomes at the top were achieved, in large part, by squeezing those below: by cutting wages, slashing benefits, crushing unions, and diverting a rising share of national resources to financial wheeling and dealing...Perhaps more important still, the wealthy exert a vastly disproportionate effect on policy. And elite priorities — obsessive concern with budget deficits, with the supposed need to slash social programs — have done a lot to deepen [wage stagnation and income inequality]."
[90] https://www.youtube.com/watch?v=nHFTtz3uucY
[91] https://www.thenation.com/article/donald-trumps-rise-has-coincided-with-an-explosion-of-hate-groups/
[92] https://theintercept.com/2017/08/15/donald-trump-has-been-a-racist-all-his-life-and-he-isnt-going-to-change-after-charlottesville/
[93] http://www.latimes.com/nation/politics/la-na-pol-trump-lebron-james-20180804-story.html
[94] https://www.theatlantic.com/politics/archive/2016/03/who-are-donald-trumps-supporters-really/471714/
[95] https://www.theatlantic.com/politics/archive/2016/03/who-are-donald-trumps-supporters-really/471714/
[96] https://www.theatlantic.com/notes/2016/01/what-bernie-sanders-and-donald-trump-have-in-common/422907/
[97] http://www.foxnews.com/politics/2017/01/16/trump-reportedly-insists-healthcare-replacement-will-have-insurance-for-everybody.html
[98] https://www.forbes.com/sites/chuckjones/2018/07/08/trumps-and-chinas-tariffs-could-do-

permanent-damage-to-soybean-farmers/#682dedc97287

[99] https://www.cnbc.com/2018/03/07/heres-how-congress-can-stop-trumps-tariffs--if-lawmakers-want-to.html

[100] https://www.businessinsider.com/trump-tariffs-trade-war-great-depression-mistake-2018-5

[101] https://www.cnbc.com/2018/07/24/trump-plans-to-give-billions-in-aid-to-farmers-hurt-by-tariffs-report.html

[102] https://www.huffingtonpost.com/henry-rosemont-jr/no-republican-family-values_b_11109560.html

[103] https://www.newsweek.com/roy-moore-all-nine-accusers-allegations-summaries-713744

[104] https://www.theguardian.com/us-news/2017/nov/21/donald-trump-roy-moore-sexual-misconduct-allegations

[105] Again, Trump's relentless, adoring support for Putin's false claim of no Russian interference is in direct contradiction to the unanimous conclusion of the U.S. intelligence agencies that Russia in fact hacked the 2016 election in support of Trump's candidacy. https://www.huffingtonpost.com/entry/senate-intel-committee-russia-meddling-2016-election_us_5b3c4af2e4b05127cced824b

[106] http://discourseinprogress.com/on-the-origins-of-one-person-one-vote/

[107] The greatest danger Alexis De Tocqueville saw was that public opinion would become an all-powerful force, and that the majority could tyrannize unpopular minorities and marginal individuals. "Democracy in America". Right now we actually have that premise turned upside down. A tyrannical minority.

[108] https://www.youtube.com/watch?v=WJlY9C7YWzI

[109] https://www.mediamatters.org/blog/2016/12/01/comprehensive-guide-alex-jones-conspiracy-theorist-and-trump-valuable-asset/214668

[110] https://www.autostraddle.com/this-is-how-fox-news-brainwashes-its-viewers-our-in-depth-investigation-of-the-propaganda-cycle-297107/; http://www.chicagotribune.com/entertainment/tv/ct-fox-news-military-analyst-quits-20180320-story.html

[111] https://variety.com/2018/tv/news/sinclair-promos-backlash-1202741019/

[112] Alex Jones, whom Donald Trump consistently promotes, along with his baseless claims, is the most notably outrageous conspiracy theorist. See https://www.npr.org/sections/thetwo-way/2018/04/17/603223968/sandy-hook-parents-sue-conspiracy-theorist-alex-jones-over-claim-shooting-was-fa and https://www.youtube.com/watch?v=MzIOidaeFC0

[113] https://www.huffingtonpost.com/entry/russian-trolls-fake-news_us_58dde6bae4b08194e3b8d5c4

[114] https://www.washingtonpost.com/news/opinions/wp/2016/11/28/trump-just-proved-hes-a-pathological-liar-which-part-is-worse-the-lying-or-the-pathology/?noredirect=on&utm_term=.b7ceb653a05e

[115] 115 https://variety.com/2018/tv/news/sinclair-promos-backlash-1202741019/

[116] https://en.wikipedia.org/wiki/United_States_presidential_election_in_Florida,_2000

[117] https://en.wikipedia.org/wiki/List_of_federal_judges_appointed_by_George_W._Bush

[118] https://www.thenation.com/article/why-invasion-iraq-was-single-worst-foreign-policy-decision-american-history/

[119] http://time.com/3445010/ruth-bader-ginsburg-citizens-united/

[120] https://www.essence.com/2013/06/25/sound-supreme-court-weakens-voting-rights-act

[121] https://www.motherjones.com/politics/2011/12/leadup-iraq-war-timeline/

[122] https://www.snopes.com/fact-check/a-word-transformed/

[123] https://www.motherjones.com/politics/2011/12/leadup-iraq-war-timeline/

[124]http://www.slate.com/articles/news_and_politics/politics/2016/05/a_letter_to_a_bernie_o r_bust_voter.html

[125] https://www.nbcnews.com/news/world/guess-who-came-dinner-flynn-putin-n742696

[126] https://fivethirtyeight.com/features/jill-stein-democratic-spoiler-or-scapegoat/

[127] http://time.com/4403367/1968-dnc-convention-protest-photos/

[128] https://www.huffingtonpost.com/entry/kirsten-gillibrand-al-franken-2020_us_5b58994ae4b0b15aba945e79

[129] https://www.huffingtonpost.com/fred-wertheimer/citizens-united-and-its-d_b_8979252.html

[130] https://www.bloomberg.com/politics/graphics/2016-presidential-campaign-fundraising/

[131]https://www.realclearpolicy.com/articles/2017/06/29/deconstructing_the_administrative_ state_110284.html; https://www.cnn.com/2017/03/30/politics/trump-bannon-administrative-state/index.html

[132] https://www.theatlantic.com/politics/archive/2017/12/blowing-up-the-deficit-is-part-of-the-plan/548720/

[133] http://fortune.com/2017/02/25/bannon-trump-cabinet-cpac/; https://www.usatoday.com/story/news/politics/2017/01/12/some-trump-cabinet-picks-skeptical-their-agencies-missions/96417756/

[134] http://time.com/4598910/rick-perry-department-energy-oops-gaffe/

[135] https://www.motherjones.com/kevin-drum/2017/02/donald-trump-hangs-australia-threatens-invade-mexico/

[136] https://www.independent.co.uk/news/world/americas/us-politics/donald-trump-angela-merkel-shake-hand-refuse-a7635911.html

[137] http://www.nydailynews.com/news/politics/trump-shoves-montenegro-prime-minister-nato-base-article-1.3195449

[138] http://thinkexist.com/quotation/-if_you_tell_a_lie_big_enough_and_keep_repeating/345877.html

[139] http://thinkexist.com/quotation/-if_you_tell_a_lie_big_enough_and_keep_repeating/345877.html

[140] https://www.weeklystandard.com/vanity-fair-trump-kept-a-volume-of-hitlers-speeches-by-his-bedside/article/2001343

[141] Most recently this was the result of the Democrats staying home during the 2010 midterm elections allowing Republicans to take control of a majority of the state legislatures. In most states those legislatures are empowered with the responsibility of redistricting. This is particularly important every ten years (e.g. 2010, 2020) since this is when the national census is taken. For an analysis on the effect in the 2016 elections see https://www.mlive.com/news/index.ssf/2017/06/ap_analysis_shows_how_gerryman.html

[142] https://newrepublic.com/article/143598/real-voter-fraud-trump-investigates-illegal-votes-states-rush-to-limit-access-ballot-box

[143] We should have passed legislation allowing more infrastructure spending recommended by President Obama early in the recovery from the Great Recession. (It is true that immediate bipartisan legislation and efforts helped turn around the recovery. See e.g. https://www.economy.com/mark-zandi/documents/End-of-Great-Recession.pdf) I strongly feel our stimulus package should have been much larger and should have included a major infrastructure component. It would have been truly affordable at that time when unemployment was sky high. The Republican Congress thwarted President Obama's efforts in this regard. The Trump/Republican trillion-dollar tax break passed last year obliterated any chance we had for a more modest infrastructure plan.

[144] https://truecostblog.com/2009/08/09/countries-with-universal-healthcare-by-date/

[145] https://www.forbes.com/sites/theapothecary/2011/10/20/how-a-conservative-think-tank-

invented-the-individual-mandate/#76f1d38c6187
146http://www.slate.com/blogs/the_slatest/2015/02/20/giuliani_obama_doesn_t_love_americ
a_white_mother_grandparents_cited.html
147 https://www.cfr.org/experts/richard-n-haass
148 *The Mike Pence Show*,1999
149 Pence Campaign website
150 I was originally motivated to write this "pamphlet" when I recalled the historic work, *Common Sense,* by Thomas Payne. I felt Donald Trump's coarse and dangerously autocratic temperament was the greatest threat to our country that I had witnessed in my lifetime, exceeding Joe McCarthy's vile and baseless Communist witch hunt in the 50's and the break-in and cover up of the Nixon Era. It just felt that the Trump Presidency was a crisis unparalleled since the revolt against the British Crown and the creation of our Constitution.
151 https://www.rollingstone.com/politics/politics-news/the-dark-twisted-failure-of-devin-nunes-202154/; https://www.washingtonexaminer.com/devin-nunes-hometown-paper-accuses-him-of-doing-the-dirty-work-to-protect-trump
152 https://www.washingtontimes.com/news/2018/jan/30/john-heilemann-suggests-devin-nunes-russian-agent/
153 https://www.usatoday.com/story/opinion/2018/04/11/paul-ryan-retire-editorials-debates/507367002/
154 "The price good men pay for indifference to public affairs is to be ruled by evil men." Plato; "One of the penalties for refusing to participate in politics is that you end up being governed by your inferiors. – Plato
155 "Democracy is the worst form of government, except for all the others." Winston Churchill

156 https://en.wikipedia.org/wiki/The_Emperor%27s_New_Clothes
157 It's fascinating to note that in almost all of his "negotiations" with foreign leaders and envoys Trump has backtracked and capitulated his bargaining position. See e.g. *Fareed's Take* in the start of the following youtube link:
https://www.youtube.com/watch?v=14eI_05wKQ0 See also
https://www.yahoo.com/news/trumps-artless-deals-world-stage-154223248.html. Another common tactic of Trump's charades in the international negotiation sphere is to preposterously declare victory after a non-event. After his summit with Kim Jong Un Trump announced that North Korea "is no longer a nuclear threat."
http://www.nydailynews.com/news/world/ny-news-trump-korea-threat-20180613-story.html
158 https://www.esquire.com/news-politics/a50069/nobody-does-it-better-than-donald-trump/
159 *1984* written by George Orwell in 1948
160 https://www.themorgan.org/exhibitions/the-great-experiment
161 https://www.brainyquote.com/quotes/barack_obama_409128
162 https://www.independent.co.uk/news/people/barack-obama-fired-up-ready-to-go-speech-new-hampshire-a7404171.html